MW01101971

I

Special Acknowledgements:

To my wonderful wife and children, I want to offer my deepest gratitude. You not only had to put up with the time it takes to write a book, but the sermons that were preached before its creation.

To my dear friend, and faithful editor, Brian Whiteside, I want to say "thank you!" You provided a quality and level of excellence that I truly admire.

To my friends and co-laborers on the Alive in Christ radio network – thank you!

To the men who have labored before me – Dr. Gary Martin, Rev. Fred Seidler, Rev. David Young and Rev. Danny Dickson – you have given me a view to godliness and stand indelibly marked in my mind as the highest examples of faithful men.

To the faithful members of Mountain View Baptist Church: You have proved time and again how deeply rooted you are in Biblical truth and the love of Jesus Christ. Thank you.

And, ultimately, I want to thank my Lord Jesus Christ who has called me into His service to build His kingdom for His glory. Amen.

What others are saying

I was hooked on Michael Duncan's latest book, *From Vision to Victory*, from the opening story in chapter one that highlights a modern island ritual called the Jungle Run to the very end when he challenged his readers to consider if the victories in our lives have been such that no one could tell they were done by God, in which case, we are not yet living in the victory God intended for us.

Along the way Michael uses the story of Nehemiah to help us understand God's provision, the reality of facing persecution for our beliefs, the need to set right priorities and the importance of prayer. Through this fresh look at the ancient biblical story of Nehemiah, readers learn how to discover God's vision for their lives and then move from mere vision to the reality of that vision fulfilled. I recommend this book to anyone, but especially to those who are looking for a new purpose in life.

- DR. TERRY DORSETT, Pastor/Director, Next Generation Evangelistic Network author of *Mission Possible: Reaching the Next Generation for Christ* and *Teaming Up: Using our Spiritual Gifts Effectively*

~~~

From Vision to Victory is the must read pastoral leadership book for 2014. What Michael Duncan offers is a refreshing look at Nehemiah's pastoral leadership. As a military officer, achieving a hard-fought victory is relatively easy in a "products and projects" "get the job done" operational environment. However, as the unit chaplain, I often feel like a round peg in a square hole attempting to successfully perform relationship-centric ministries in a products and projects driven atmosphere. *From Vision to Victory* stopped me in my tracks when Michael challenged me to see that God had a lot more in mind for Nehemiah than just building a wall.

- CAPT. ROY BUTLER, U.S. Army Chaplain, Author of *American Politics and the Burden of Voting*

~~~

From Vision to Victory

The Nehemiah Project

Other books by Michael Duncan

Starting Out: A Study Guide for New Believers

The Discipling Church: Encouraging, Equipping and
Empowering the Body of Christ (With Tony Marino, Dr. Jeff
Klick and Brian Whiteside)

A Life Worth Living (Booklet)

Shadows: Book of Aleth, Part One

Revelation: Book of Aleth, Part Two

Shadow Remnant

From Vision to Victory
The Nehemiah Project

Michael Duncan

From Vision to Victory
The Nehemiah Project

Copyright © 2014 by Michael Duncan

ISBN-13: 978-1496030535

ISBN-10: 1496030532

Therefore, my dear brothers, stand firm. Let nothing move you. Always give yourselves fully to the work of the Lord, because you know that your labor in the Lord is not in vain.

IN with messiah
and by King Jesus

~ 1 Corinthians 15:58

IX

Contents

2014 ∴ 36+ years ministry

Foreword

Leadership from God

Over the past 30+years of ministry I have watched many pastors and church leaders attempt to inspire their people to accomplish great and lofty goals. Some have tried to motivate their people with catchy slogans and slick marketing strategies. Others choose grandiose visions that they have dreamed accompanied by ominous overtones should they fail to achieve it. And others love to pick spectacular numbers as their goal to achieve as if going for the impossible is the most inspirational of all.

Many churches hit their targets through much perseverance and constant reminders, and most try to give all the glory to God when they succeed. But I am rarely convinced that God was the initiator of the vision nor was He the enabler to help them achieve it. Maybe this is cynical or judgmental, but I have been around long enough to watch actual results over the years. Many of these churches grow larger, their staff and their activities increase, their community profile is enhanced, but there is little to no impact on their neighborhoods, towns or cities. The divorce rates in their own congregations remain unchanged, there is no increase in those being inspired and called into full time ministry, and the surrounding communities have no sense of the power of God to change lives inside the walls of their churches.

I like the insights Michael has penned in *"From Vision to Victory: The Nehemiah Project"*. He has taken time to see from a leaders' perspective, what it takes to lead God's people to accomplish God's directives. I hesitate to use the word "goals" as I don't believe God functions by successfully achieving a list of goals. God has divine plans He seeks to accomplish through His people, yet getting the attention of His people in the first place is God's greatest challenge.

Unfortunately, despite what churches claim, most seem greatly disoriented to God today. Few know how to "seek and search for God with all of their heart" anymore. Most are competing with social media or other more 'progressive' congregations, and have lost touch with some of the very core elements of what it means to be in a relationship with God. Congregational prayer is almost non-existent. Fasting is out of style. Repentance, reconciliation, and confession are terms found only in dusty books detailing revivals in generations past. *From Vision to Victory* reminds us of what the basics are in the Christian life and recalls the tried and true ways of God with His people that guarantee God's pleasure and power at work in and through His people.

We can have success in our own eyes, but if we want to impact eternity, if we want to see lives transformed by the power of God, if we want to see the little we have to offer expand and explode powerfully in our surrounding communities, we need to repent, turn back to God, and truly follow Him.

DR. TOM BLACKABY writer, author, speaker

International Director for Blackaby Ministries International

XVI

Introduction
Finding the Vision

"So then, King Agrippa, I was not disobedient to the vision from heaven." ~ Acts 26:19

THE FUNDAMENTAL REALITY of the Christian life is not the Christian's activity for the Kingdom of God but God's activity in the midst of the Christian's experience. With this in mind, one of the greatest hindrances to the work of the Kingdom of God is the busy nature of God's people without consulting God first. Frustrations, doubt, despair, discouragement, all these feelings will be experienced as a result of not knowing if a project originates from the heart of God or of men. Many good projects have been dreamed up by men and have failed simply for the lack of God's presence and His leadership in the process. We must have a vision, a direction or directive from God, before we venture into the realm of Kingdom work.

Our Lord Jesus didn't work on His own initiative; He did everything that He saw His Father doing. Jesus said in

John 5:19, "I tell you the truth, the Son can do nothing by himself; he can do only what he sees his Father doing, because whatever the Father does the Son also does." At the last supper with His disciples Jesus prayed, "I have brought you [the Father] glory on earth by completing the work you gave me to do" (John 17:4). Jesus was not concerned about accomplishing those things that would magnify Himself, but those things that identified Him with the Father. Everything Jesus did was built upon the relationship that He had with His Father.

Jesus is our example for doing what God wants us to do. The disciples understood this, "To this you were called, because Christ suffered for you, leaving you an example, that you should follow in his steps" (1 Peter 2:21). Jesus declared this to the disciples when, after washing their feet, He said, "I have set you an example that you should do as I have done for you" (John 13:15). It is imperative, then, that every believer becomes deeply rooted in their relationship with Jesus to be able to understand the activity of God.

Jesus said that He reveals the purposes of God to those who are His friends: "You are my friends if you do what I command. I no longer call you servants, because a servant does not know his master's business. Instead, I have called you friends, for everything that I learned from my Father I have made known to you" (John 15:14-15). This is what it takes for every believer in Jesus to have a "vision" of the activity of God. God desires to reveal His activity to all who call upon Him. Those who remain close to Jesus, living their life in obedience to His word from a heart of love, will invariably come to know what the Father's will is. Romans 12:1-2 affirms this: "Therefore, I urge you, brothers, in view of God's mercy, to offer your bodies as living sacrifices, holy and pleasing to God—this is your spiritual act of worship. Do not conform any longer to the pattern of this world, but be transformed by the renewing of your mind. Then you will be able to test and approve what God's will is—his good, pleasing and perfect will."

Have you ever wondered what God expects, or what it takes to accomplish God's vision when He reveals it? The story of Nehemiah, and the project that God purposed for him in rebuilding the wall of Jerusalem, is an example of what God expects when He reveals His vision to His people. In the story of Nehemiah we find an ordinary man whom God called upon to do extraordinary things. God placed this project in the heart of Nehemiah (Nehemiah 2:12b). What comes next is what it takes for a man to go from vision to victory, to go from receiving God's revelation to the accomplishment of that revelation. Remember, God's first purpose for everyone is a relationship with Him in Christ Jesus. Out of that relationship God will put in the heart of

4

faithful believers the projects that He wants to accomplish through them. *With in and by them*

As you read the following pages, I encourage you to reflect upon your relationship with Christ. What is He doing in and around you? What projects has He placed before you and are you willing to respond to His leadership in your life? Remember, this is more than just doing something for God; this is doing something that God alone has purposed for you, and that God desires to accomplish through you.

Points to Ponder:

What frustrations or doubts do you experience when it comes to the work of God? *Different Definitions of the Life of following Jesus and*

Do you work to magnify yourself or to glorify God? *Honor and Re-present God the Father out of Union in Jesus*

What do you see God doing in and around you right now?

Father is hovering around me an in me and upon me to seek His Face by thoughts that center on His Name Words of Jesus which live in my by Jesus' Second self whom I depend on to Keep my soul in living Contact with Living Love Light from His Loving Tender Joyful Presence

Father is answering the prayer of Jesus whom we have in John 17. That We become a Warrior Bride, Welcoming Contending for

inspired Proclamation by Proxy & could on earth in Heaven

From Vision to Victory

Chapter One:
A Passion for God

His disciples remembered that it is written: "Zeal for your house will consume me." ~ John 2:17

Passion
and Father's
Vision Lived

From Vision to Victory

I WAS FIFTEEN years old. At this time in my life I lived on a remote and sparsely populated island in the middle of Puget Sound, Washington. In the summers of my life activities were hard to come by that would entertain and adequately distract me from the boredom and monotony that often became the norm of teenage existence. Suffice it to say, my sitting around the house all weekend long, to my parents, proved to be more taxing on them than on me — so out I went! Often I was ushered out of the house with the notion that a young man needed to be outside on such fine summer days.

On one of these particular days, the young people of the island gathered together for a common summer ritual — a "jungle run." Let me explain. A jungle run was a group of teenagers starting at one end of the island running as fast as possible to the other end of the island. It was forbidden to use any of the island's roads for this contest so the various courses chosen in this ritual consisted of scrambling headlong for about a mile through dense forest underbrush and high grassy fields. With the group assembled and ready to go we began the long and laborious journey through the island's jungle-like terrain.

As usual, I found myself on the trailing end of this assemblage of young adventurers. As I pressed on through the dense forest I watched the figures of all the other teenage boys disappear into the foliage of a million different kinds of forest vegetation. Within a short time, however, as I pressed on, with little hope of actual victory, I was startled to see the group of young men standing still about fifty yards ahead of me in the underbrush. I couldn't believe my eyes! The other competitors were stalled at the largest wall of blackberry bushes that ever existed on the earth. They looked this way and that hoping to find a path or avenue around this version of the "Great Wall." However, no amount of hoping revealed a passage through this vast and seemingly insurmountable barrier.

So, at full speed, I plunged into this thorn-infested patch and forced my way through to the end of the race! All concern for injury was lost and only one thing stayed in my mind—I was going to WIN! As I crossed the agreed upon finish line, I looked behind me to see all the other competitors following in my path. I was victorious, and it was my absolute desire for victory that propelled me to take the greatest risk. As all the other young men looked at and lamented over their cuts and scrapes from the blackberry thorns, someone in the crowd gasped and pointed at my legs. I looked down only to see them covered in blood from the hem of my khaki shorts to the tops of my tennis shoes! Moreover, my arms were drenched in sweat and blood — but I didn't mind. The sacrifice was worth it, if only for this one time.

Victory in the Christian life is not something that simply happens as we wait casually in our bedchambers for the Lord to send fire down from heaven. But for many believers today Christianity has become a passive religion that is casual and bereft of passion. If we are going to go from vision to victory in our Christian life it must be said of us that we are a people passionate for the Lord.

Look to the example of Nehemiah. When Hanani came to him with the news of the broken down walls of Jerusalem and the disheartened attitude of the remnant of God's people who lived there, this was the catalyst God used to instill into Nehemiah's heart the vision of rebuilding the wall of Jerusalem. Consider Nehemiah's reaction in Nehemiah 1:4: "When I heard these things, I sat down and wept. For some days I mourned and fasted and prayed before the God of heaven." This is not the reaction of an apathetic soul! This is the reaction of a man deeply and passionately grieved by the condition of God's people and the reality of what had happened.

However, Nehemiah's passion was not the passion of the humanitarian. No, Nehemiah was fueled with passion for the Lord God of heaven. Many will look at the plight of the human condition and be stirred in their soul with sympathy. Nehemiah knew that God's judgment was righteous and that the people of God had rebelled against the Lord (Nehemiah 1:7). Thus, he went to the only source of hope and help for the distress of his people. Nehemiah went to the Lord. We have many humanitarian causes across the face of this earth. I am not downplaying the necessity of striving to better the conditions of those who suffer, but the first passion that every believer must have is a passion for Christ. At the heart of Nehemiah's passion was the restoration of the majesty of God's name through the redemption of God's people (Nehemiah 1:9-10).

The passion of Nehemiah, the passion of Paul, the passion of every man and woman of God who is stirred in their heart to accomplish God's purpose is a passion for God Himself. God said, "My name will be great among the nations, from the rising to the setting of the sun" (Malachi

1:11). God is seeking hearts that are completely His (2 Chronicles 16:9). The overwhelming disposition of the modern Christian life is that it is all about the individual and not about God. God does not save for our glory but for His. God does not call us for our glory but for His. It is when believers are consumed with glorifying God that they will discover the passion that will carry them from vision to victory. However, rather than just lamenting the prevailing attitude, it is imperative that you see the solution to the problem of indifference. God wants you to have a heart of passion for Him and His work.

When was the last time God stirred in your heart a desire for His name to be great? Do you recall a time when you knew that God had spoken to you concerning the restoration of His people? Bill McCartney was moved to restore God's name among Christian men and Promise Keepers was born. God moved in the heart of John Wesley and the Methodist movement began. Martin Luther was stirred in his soul and the Reformation found a voice. Evan Roberts prayed "O God, bend me" and the nation of Wales was never the same. In each instance, God moved in the hearts of His people who were ready for His presence to move them from mere spectators to leaders.

From Vision to Victory

A Continual Love Relationship with Christ

When faced with the drama, tragedy and pathetic condition
of the people in Jerusalem, and the condition of Jerusalem
itself, Nehemiah went to the very anchor of his life — his
relationship with the Living God. Every person, great and
small, when faced with the tempests of life will ultimately
run to the one relationship that gives them the most
satisfaction and comfort. Some relate to a bottle of alcohol,
some to drugs, some to sexual encounters, some to friends or
family, etc. The crisis moments of life reveal what people
rely upon for strength.

Consider, for a moment, the last crisis that occurred
or the last trial that you needed to overcome. When you
faced that crisis did you stand? Were you alone? Who did
you turn to? You will find that the relationship you treasure
most is the one that you will ultimately seek out when the
storms of life come. When Nehemiah came face to face with
the tragedy of Jerusalem his first response was to pray. He
sought the one true relationship that he could depend on.

Nehemiah 1:4-11 reveals the heart-cry of this man.
You cannot help but discover his understanding of God.
Nehemiah knew God as "O LORD" the "God of heaven" the
"great and awesome God." Consider for a moment your
times of prayer and the manner in which you address the

13

Almighty Creator. I find that in my own experience I speak to God far too casually. Many believers pray to God as if they were addressing a letter to a distant friend: "Dear God." It should be that believers take their times of prayer as if they were breathing in the very atmosphere of heaven itself. Today's passion of love for the Savior is far too cool and, in comparison with Scripture, practically cold.

Now it's "continual" for a reason. Many will equate their relationship with the Lord Jesus to some experience that happened in the distant past. That is, many will say they know Him because they "walked an aisle" or "signed a decision card." Some will say they were baptized in a certain church or prayed a prayer when they were young. These are not wrong things to do but a true love relationship is one that is real in the here and now.

Think about it this way. I tell you I'm married. However, you never see me with my wife. You never hear me speak about her in a crowd. You never even see me carry a picture of her. My declaration of marriage is: I signed a card (marriage license), I walked an aisle, I prayed a prayer (said my vows), and I was even in church when I did all those things. The problem is there is no evidence outside my testimony verifying the things that I am saying. I either have no true marriage or I have no desire for the marriage I am in.

From Vision to Victory

True victory in the life of a believer is borne out of a passionate relationship with the Savior who loves us. It is not something that you strive to attain, but rather is something that wellsprings from the continual love relationship you have with Him. God could move in the heart of Nehemiah for His purpose because Nehemiah was a willing vessel, completely yielded to the will of the Father out of a deep and passionate love for Him.

Complete Cleansing through Repentance

The greatest dissipater of passion for Christ is sin. Sin, in its essence, is the allowance of a disposition to govern my life other than the person of Jesus Christ. Jesus said only one master could ever sit enthroned in the life of an individual (Matthew 6:24). Paul said this: "Those who live according to the sinful nature have their minds set on what that nature desires; but those who live in accordance with the Spirit have their minds set on what the Spirit desires" (Romans 8:5). That is to say, the controlling issue of your life is either the Spirit of Christ or sin.

Nehemiah recognized the issue surrounding the Israelites' captivity—they had rebelled against the Living God. Nehemiah 1:6b-7, "I confess the sins we Israelites, including myself, have committed against you. We have

15

acted very wickedly toward you. We have not obeyed the commands, decrees and laws you gave your servant Moses." Nehemiah fully understood for there to be any activity of God in the midst of His people, someone needed to repent. So, in complete identification with his entire nation, Nehemiah cried out to God in confession.

How many people today are more willing to "point and blame" than to "identify and confess?" The great issue that plagues most modern thinking is that no one wants to be the one to blame. We have doctors and lawyers and specialists of every kind that are willing to declare a person innocent of the issues that are in his or her life. As an example of this, consider "no fault" divorces. Many today are not drunkards; they have a disease called alcoholism. Unruly children don't get disciplined; they get drugged. Criminals cite poor upbringing. Time and again the sinner is never confronted with sin. Nehemiah flies in the face of the modern thinking of litigation and declares openly his guilt and the guilt of the entire nation before God.

The fact is; to love God is to hate sin. The discovery of a passionate heart for God requires the abandonment of a sinful life for the righteousness of Christ. Proverbs 28:13 states, "He who conceals his sins does not prosper, but whoever confesses and renounces them finds mercy." The path that God has given for freedom is the path of repentance. Follow the path that the Lord has laid out and you find yourself walking in the right direction. A simple proverb: "If you keep doing what you've always done, you'll keep getting what you've always got." It requires change and repentance to bring your life into the pathway of God's purpose.

Confidence in the promises of God

True passion for Christ and His work comes through relationship, and that relationship is built upon your firm trust and confidence in the promises of God. Consider again Nehemiah's prayer. Verses eight and nine reveal his understanding of what God had promised would happen and what God has promised could happen. "Remember the instructions you gave your servant Moses, saying, 'If you are unfaithful, I will scatter you among the nations.'" Nehemiah was living in the fulfillment of that very thing. There was no doubt in his mind that what God had said would happen, happened. The children of Israel were captive; the city of Jerusalem was left in ruins; the remnant remaining in Judah was in great trouble and disgrace. Nehemiah understood that because of the sin of the children of Israel, they were suffering exile in a foreign land. Everything God spoke came to pass. Nehemiah knew God had fulfilled His word.

From Vision to Victory

Once Nehemiah acknowledged God fulfilling His promise, his next step was a step of faith. It is easy to say that God is faithful when you live in the fulfillment of a promise, but what about the promises that have yet come to pass? Nehemiah continued praying, reciting God's own word: "But if you return to me and obey my commands, then even if your exiled people are at the farthest horizon, I will gather them from there and bring them to the place I have chosen as a dwelling for my Name." Nehemiah not only knew the promises of God, he knew the God of the promises. He knew God would never speak a word He was unable or unwilling to fulfill. God would honor His own word, and for Nehemiah that was enough to believe. Nehemiah brought his faith in line with God's promise of restoration because he knew God and knew that God was faithful.

How do you understand God? Confidence in the promises of God comes from confidence in the character of God. A promise is only as good as the one who makes it. So to believe God is perfect in all His ways is to believe every one of His promises are reliable. In 2 Corinthians 1:20 this reality is clearly revealed: "For no matter how many promises God has made, they are 'Yes' in Christ. And so through him the 'Amen' is spoken by us to the glory of God." The qualifying reality for the fulfillment of God's promises is for the believer to be found "in Christ." Anyone who remains outside a relationship with Christ Jesus remains outside God's promises.

Look to your life and see if God is attempting to gain your attention for His purposes. I would imagine that He is. God has a purpose for each Christian and accompanying that purpose is a promise that will deliver victory. God told Moses to go and deliver His people out of slavery. God gave Joshua the charge of leading Israel into the Promised Land. David was anointed king over all Israel. Paul was appointed as the apostle for the Gentiles. In each instance, what God had commanded He fulfilled. The ultimate test for the believer is whether or not to trust in the God who has given His word. God promised each individual mentioned above that He would be with them, that He would go before them and protect them and guide them and provide for them. With the security of God's promise these men went forth and gained victory.

Nehemiah knew God had given him the call to go forward and rebuild the wall of Jerusalem. However, for Nehemiah to find the courage and passion to go forward with this vision he needed to understand God's promise for the restoration of Jerusalem. Thus he prayed in response to his comprehension of God's promises and then went forward with God. Nehemiah didn't go forward with the project because it was a good idea, but because it was God's idea. Nehemiah had to rely completely on God's promise to bring to completion the project God purposed.

This is true for every believer. Until you trust completely that God will do what He said He would do, you will ultimately lack passion and courage to go forward in God's vision for your life. Consider this word from Romans 4:20-21, "Yet he [Abraham] did not waver through unbelief regarding the promise of God, but was strengthened in his faith and gave glory to God, being fully persuaded that God had power to do what he had promised." Are you "fully persuaded?" Do you waiver through unbelief? Jesus said, "Everything is possible for him who believes" (Mark 9:23). This does not mean that I can do anything I desire, but that God's purpose is fully realized through the life of faith. If God has given you a promise concerning His purpose in your life, allow that promise to well up in you the courage and passion to go forward in faith and do that which God has given you.

This prayer of Nehemiah does not build the passion in his heart – it reveals it. Nehemiah knew and experienced a deep love relationship with God that produced in him a desire for God's purposes to be fulfilled in his life. His prayer reveals the inner workings of his heart toward God. Nehemiah lived in a continual love relationship with God Almighty. He knew God for who He is and for what He does. Nehemiah also knew the ramifications of sin and that the only way to deal with sin is through God's complete cleansing. This cleansing comes through confession and repentance. Nehemiah trusted God completely and knew God would fulfill His promise. He lived in the fulfillment of the promise of Judgment, he trusted God for the promise of restoration.

The passion of your life is built upon your relationship with Christ Jesus. If there is no passion for God and His activity, examine your life and re-evaluate your relationship with Him. Commit your life by faith, confess your sin, and stand confident upon God's promises to begin your move from vision to victory.

Points to Ponder:

Do you have a continual love relationship with God?

Do you seek God's cleansing through confession and repentance of sin?

Do you confidently stand upon God's promises?

From Vision to Victory

Chapter Two: Finding the Plan of God

"For I know the plans I have for you," declares the LORD, "plans to prosper you and not to harm you, plans to give you hope and a future.' ~ Jeremiah 29:11

From Vision to Victory

A MODERN DAY proverb goes something like this: "People don't plan to fail, they fail to plan." Books, tapes, lectures, seminars and conferences speak continually of the need to organize and administrate the work that is necessary for the accomplishment of a plethora of ideas and goals. True, planning is essential in the achievement of personal or corporate goals — but what about spiritual visions? Shouldn't the believer simply be free to experience the unencumbered nature of faith? Oswald Chamber's philosophy of "trust God and do the next thing"[1] is often replaced with the notion of "trust God and do nothing." It is imperative for the achievement of victory that plans are made.

---

[1] McCasland, David, Oswald Chambers: *Abandoned to God* (Grand Rapids: Discovery House Publishers, 1993), 229

One of the great dangers, however, is the danger of making plans according to your own design. When God grants a vision of His purpose, you must understand that He also has a plan for accomplishing it. Rather than develop, the believer must discover God's plans for His vision. Consider Abraham. God gave Abraham (then Abram) an understanding of His purpose. In Genesis chapter 15, God promised Abram a son. From that offspring, God would make Abram's descendants as numerous as the stars. Verse six says, "Abram believed the Lord, and he credited it to him as righteousness." Abram believed God, but then attempted to accomplish the vision with human ingenuity. In Genesis chapter 16, Abram and Sarai decided to take matters into their own hands, so Abram slept with the handmaid, Hagar. From this union Ishmael was conceived and along with that came thousands of years of unremitting hostility between Isaac and Ishmael.

Down through the ages the people of God have tried to accomplish the vision of God according to the plans of men. Moses tried to free Israel one Egyptian at a time (see Exodus 2:12); David tried to bring the Ark of the Covenant back to Jerusalem by his own method (see 2 Samuel 6); Peter would have kept Christ from the cross (see Matthew 16:22). The full scope of God's purpose is beyond the comprehension of men, yet men still try and accomplish

God's purpose with human planning. The plans concerning God's vision must be from God. Jeremiah 29:11 states: "I know the plans that I have for you..." God alone knows how to accomplish His purposes, so God must be the one who draws up the plans. To act according to our own design and still hope to function in the will of God ultimately leads to frustration and failure because, "Many are the plans in a man's heart, but it is the Lord's purpose that prevails" (Proverbs 19:21).

If you do God's work according to God's plan you will find yourself on the right path for God's victory in your life. In this chapter there are four discoveries from Nehemiah that will help you understand how to discover God's plan for accomplishing His vision.

Take Time to Prepare

There is a tendency today, in this hurry-up world, to make activity and busyness the symbols of success and the hallmark for God's involvement. In today's electronic, information age, where data can be transmitted at mind-boggling speeds, it is assumed the human ability to process information and determine the proper course of action should be just as fast. Fast food, fast cars, faster internet speeds, microwaves, etc. are all signs revealing the desire to maximize the level of activity in a minimal amount of time. Nevertheless, God does not operate on the time schedules of men. To get at God's plan requires a life that is willing to be patient.

One of the greatest difficulties in Christian work is patience. You catch a vision from God and are immediately ready to venture into the great unknown of spiritual activity. There is wisdom, however, in taking time to prepare. Proverbs 19:2 states: "It is not good to have zeal without knowledge, nor to be hasty and miss the way." Many good Christians, with good intentions and a passion for Christ, have sensed God's calling or experienced a passionate vision for service, but run headlong into disaster simply because they didn't take the necessary time to prepare.

For Nehemiah, this point is clearly understood from the simple phrase, "in the month of Nisan" (Nehemiah 2:1). The fact is Nehemiah waited four months from the time Hanani reported to him concerning the status of Jerusalem (Nehemiah 1:1) to the time he approached King Artaxerxes. Undoubtedly, those four months were spent in personal preparation for the events that were to unfold in his life.

Far too often Christians will run ahead of themselves and God in order to get to work. The greatest work, and the work that will reap the greatest reward, is the work that is spent in preparation for the journey. To illustrate this, consider the expedition of Amundsen the Norwegian explorer.

In 1911, Amundsen set off on an incredible journey to become the first man to reach the South Pole. Before setting foot on the cold wastelands of Antarctica, Amundsen painstakingly prepared for the journey. He studied the method of the Eskimos and other experienced Arctic dwellers. He planned on using dog sleds so he assembled a team of highly experienced expert skiers and dog handlers. His forethought and preparation for the journey gave him and his team the best advantage for reaching their goal.

Consider Moses. For forty years Moses spent his days in the courts of Pharaoh becoming a skilled administrator and leader. Then Moses spent forty years in the desert becoming familiar with the ways of God. Until Moses was properly prepared, God could not use him for the task of rescuing His people from their bondage in Egypt. Perhaps God has revealed to you a vision for His activity in your life. Before the realization of that vision, you need to prepare yourself for the work. 2 Timothy 2:20-21, "In a large house there are articles not only of gold and silver, but also of wood and clay; some are for noble purposes and some for ignoble. If a man cleanses himself from the latter, he will be an instrument for noble purposes, made holy, useful to the Master and prepared to do any good work."

Ecclesiastes 10:10 says, "If the ax is dull and its edge unsharpened, more strength is needed but skill will bring success." The time that is spent in preparation is the time that is needed to become the kind of person that God can trust with His plan. You must understand that God is looking for those who can be trusted. When God gives you a vision, it is a call to prepare.

Seek the Necessary Permission

To function in God's plan you must understand there is a structure of authority already in place. Social rebellion is never the course for the believer. Yes, there is the need to openly stand up for what is true. Courage and faithfulness to God should illuminate the believer's life. However, God has established the kingdoms and authorities that are in place for His purpose. When we function in the plan of God we must honor the authority in place. Look at two examples of this in Scripture.

The first example is Moses. In the book of Exodus, God commanded Moses to enter into Egypt and lead the people of Israel to the freedom He promised. "So now, go. I am sending you to Pharaoh to bring my people the Israelites out of Egypt" (Exodus 3:10). When God commanded Moses to go, He sent him to Pharaoh. God didn't circumvent the authority in Egypt, though He could have. When Pharaoh refused, time and time again, to let the people go, God didn't simply evacuate His people from Egypt. God convincingly demonstrated His absolute authority over Pharaoh and Pharaoh finally, reluctantly, submitted to God. The people didn't leave, however, until Pharaoh sent them away.

From this example it is important to understand that there may be opposition from the authority of this world to the activity of God. However, when God has given a vision, you must hear the encouragement of God in Habakkuk: "Though it linger, wait for it; it will certainly come and will not delay" (Habakkuk 2:3b). Often believers are eager to launch into the activity of God and there is resistance from those in authority. The action, then, is to wait on God to make the way open for His activity. Too many of God's people will carry out open revolt and protest rather than patiently wait upon the Lord to make the way. It's true, you don't disobey the word of God for the sake of men (see Acts 5:29), but allow God the opportunity to make the way open for you to fulfill His vision.

The next example I want to show you is David. David was anointed as king over Israel yet another king held the throne—Saul. After entering King Saul's service, David became well known as a man greatly used of God. In 1 Samuel chapter 24, David is on the run from the anger and murderous intent of Saul. On one particular day, David was hiding in a cave and Saul entered into the same cave to take a break. David's men encouraged him to end this senseless exile and take Saul's life. However, David knew that God had anointed Saul as king and only God had the authority to remove him. 1 Samuel 24:6, "The Lord forbid that I should do such a thing to my master, the Lord's anointed, or lift my hand against him; for he is the anointed of the Lord." David was willing to wait for God to establish him as king and not take matters into his own hands. All of God's people should take such a view of obedience to Christ. You must wait for God to establish His will in your life and not take the matter into your own hands.

We must understand that God has a better perspective and it may just be that the people in authority are there to keep us from going too far too fast. It may be that God will use you as a testimony of patience and faithfulness. Hebrews 13:17 says, "Obey your leaders and submit to their authority. They keep watch over you as men who must give an account. Obey them so that their work will be a joy, not a burden, for that would be of no advantage to you." Do you want the greatest advantage possible to accomplish the task God has given you? Be faithful to obey your leaders.

Nehemiah was diligent in seeking the necessary permission. In fact, Nehemiah spoke to two Kings that day. In verses four and five he first spoke to the King of kings. "Then I prayed to the God of heaven." Then he spoke to the king of Persia, "and I answered the king." What would have happened if Artaxerxes refused to allow the work to take place? Would Nehemiah defy the king and proceed on his own? If he did, he knew the results would be terminal. There are times believers must defy the edicts and mandates of appointed leaders, however, when that happens, every believer must be prepared to endure the consequences of that choice. For example, the disciples encountered resistance to their preaching the gospel of Jesus Christ (see Acts 5:27-41). The Sanhedrin commanded them not to speak any more in His name, and yet the command of God was to proclaim the message of truth. Earlier, the Apostles tried to persuade the ruling elders of Israel that their work was given to them by God (see Acts 4:19-20). To keep preaching required that they defy the authority of their earthly leaders. However, they also willingly endured punishment and persecution for their obedience to the Lord.

Sometimes permission cannot be obtained due to the sinfulness of the human heart and yet God is calling for you to go and do His will. When the time comes for you to be obedient to the vision, God will make the way available for you. If you cannot obtain the necessary permission, it may cost you persecution or difficulty. During those times, endure.

Examine the Project Thoroughly

For Nehemiah, after he received permission from the king, his next step was to venture to Jerusalem and see the situation for himself. Once he got there, he went from gate to gate inspecting firsthand the state of the city's walls (see Nehemiah 2:11-16). Without involving anyone or dedicating resources to the project, or even talking about it with the people that traveled with him, Nehemiah needed to know the extent of the work.

What a foolish undertaking it is to try and accomplish a great task without first knowing the extent that it will cost you. I knew of a Christian school that endeavored to launch in a community that had no Christian school. Many wanted to step right into the work, but one pastor counseled that they should wait, examine the situation, and figure out what it would really take to accomplish the goal. Not being a forceful voice on the committee, his words went unheeded and they "stepped out in faith" to do the task. Two years later, the school was closed and many hearts were hurt through the experience.

From Vision to Victory

The idea of "stepping out in faith" does not preclude the need to thoroughly examine the project. Consider the words of Jesus:

> Suppose one of you wants to build a tower. Will he not first sit down and estimate the cost to see if he has enough money to complete it? For if he lays the foundation and is not able to finish it, everyone who sees it will ridicule him, saying, "This fellow began to build and was not able to finish." Or suppose a king is about to go to war against another king. Will he not first sit down and consider whether he is able with ten thousand men to oppose the one coming against him with twenty thousand? If he is not able, he will send a delegation while the other is still a long way off and will ask for terms of peace. In the same way, any of you who does not give up everything he has cannot be my disciple. ~ Luke 14:28-33

In the matter of discipleship, Jesus calls us to count the cost before we even step into a life of obedience and faithfulness to Him. How many Christians, however, are willing to forgo the cost-counting command and simply thrust their lives into projects and endeavors that will ultimately overwhelm and overtax their own abilities and resources? They call it faith when in reality it is more likely presumption.

In my own denomination there is a practice that requires potential new pastors for a church to come and preach "in view of a call." The pastor will come, spend time with the church, attend a Sunday-School class, visit the members and preach for them on a particular Sunday morning. He will have the opportunity to be questioned by the congregation, and in turn, ask questions of the congregation. Ultimately, what the church and prospective pastor are doing is examining the project. Church planters are often asked to visit the mission field where they intend to begin a new work and "check out" the community and meet the people.

Nehemiah knew that to grasp the full nature of God's plan, he needed to understand the magnitude of the task. You might ask, "So, if Nehemiah thought the project was too big, he would have given up?" No. The issue of examining the project is not necessarily to determine if you have the ability to handle it. Nehemiah already knew that the project was commanded by God, he just examined it to know the full extent of what God had called him to do. When you step into the vision of God, it is good to know what is ahead of you. You may not be able to foresee all the potential challenges you will face, but it is of great value to the servant of Christ to know the extent of the project. In a nutshell – it's not a bad idea to know what you're getting into.

Enlist the Help of God's People

There is great value in cooperation among the people of God. This is seen, quite clearly, in the wall project of Nehemiah. As he navigated around the broken wall and burned gates of Jerusalem, Nehemiah knew that to accomplish the vision of God – to rebuild the wall – he couldn't do it alone. So, with great faith, Nehemiah presented the project to the people:

> Then I said to them, "You see the trouble we are in: Jerusalem lies in ruins, and its gates have been burned with fire. Come, let us rebuild the wall of Jerusalem, and we will no longer be in disgrace." I also told them about the gracious hand of my God upon me and what the king had said to me. ~ Nehemiah 2:17-18

So, with one heart, the people united behind Nehemiah and began to rebuild the wall of Jerusalem.

From Vision to Victory

If you want to work from vision to victory, I can tell you plainly that it will involve the people of God. Consider what is said in the book of Ephesians, "From him the whole body, joined and held together by every supporting ligament, grows and builds itself up in love, as each part does its work" (Ephesians 4:16). Within the structure of the Body of Christ is the simple fact that if the church does not work together to accomplish the work of Christ, then the work will not get done. It "grows and builds" as "each part does its work."

Now this does not mean that everyone has the same task, but it does mean that everyone needs to add to the effort in order to accomplish the vision. An illustration might be an Olympic rowing team. Though the captain of the team enlists the rowers and the coxswain steers the craft, it requires everyone to function in unity to have a chance at victory. If you think that God is calling you to fulfill a vision, you can be sure He is also calling you to enlist the aid of others.

If you are to find and function in the plan of God, then embrace these four principles. Once capturing the vision of God's purpose, take time to prepare. Make sure you're ready for the task. If called of God, you have His blessing, but you might need to consult with the authorities that are over your life. Seek the necessary permission from those who are in direct authority over the situation. Then examine the project. God is able to do abundantly more than we could ever ask, but you must count the cost. Do you have the determination to step into so great an endeavor? And finally, enlist the help of God's people. Surprisingly, even Simon helped Jesus carry the cross (Mark 15:21). You would do well to gain the support of others.

These principles will help to carry you from God's vision to His victory.

Points to Ponder:

Have you given yourself the time it takes to be fully prepared?

Who do you need to get permission from?

Have you examined the project thoroughly?

What people are around you that you need to enlist in the project?

Chapter Three:
The Provision of God

So Abraham called that place The LORD Will Provide. And to this day it is said, "On the mountain of the LORD it will be provided." ~ Genesis 22:14

From Vision to Victory

AS A YOUNG boy, living on a farm, one of the tasks given to me was to stack bales of hay for the horses and cattle. I was a small boy, only in the second grade, and trying to lift the bundled stalks was a chore beyond my strength. My older brother saw the dilemma I was in and, with a heave, moved the hay. He helped me all the rest of the day, and for that summer, until I was strong enough to endure the effort on my own. Such is the reality of working the vision of God — it will always be beyond our strength.

When we consider the activity of God in our lives, we must face the reality that if God does not provide the strength for the task and the resources to fulfill the vision, the work will not get done. This is true one hundred percent of the time. God must be the one who equips and provides for the projects He has ordained for us to do. All through

Scripture God demonstrates that He is the one that will provide the means to accomplish His will. This is seen in the life of the patriarchs: Abraham, Isaac, and Jacob. This is seen in the life of Joseph and four hundred years later in the life of Moses. God demonstrates His divine provision through the prophets and kings of the Old Testament. We see the providential hand of God in the life of the apostles as well as in the churches of the New Testament. Even at the end of time, in the book of Revelation, we find the provision of God in His protection of the saints.

Consider Abraham. In Genesis chapter 22, God tested Abraham with a great and unlikely command. He told Abraham to take his only son Isaac and offer him as a sacrifice to God. As the story unfolds, Abraham is certain that, somehow, God will provide deliverance for his son—and God does.

> Abraham looked up and there in a thicket he saw a ram caught by its horns. He went over and took the ram and sacrificed it as a burnt offering instead of his son. So Abraham called that place The LORD Will Provide. And to this day, it is said, "On the mountain of the LORD it will be provided" ~ Genesis 22:13-14

41

To use this example further, ask yourself, "What is the mountain of the Lord?" It is the mountain of faith, climbed by those who are willing to take God's vision for their life and strive after it with unyielding determination. Those who remain in the valley of unwillingness will never experience the provision of God for they will not climb the rugged terrain. Much like a mountain climb, the path of faithfulness takes grit, courage and the abandonment of the easy road for a much higher view.

There is a tendency today, however, to try and produce divine results by human ingenuity. Many church growth books, seminars, conferences, and ideas seem to center around the principles of marketing and demographic research. Revivalists use emotionalism and theatrics to produce results. Churches turn to "special effects" during their worship services such as extravagant video graphics and high-powered orchestration to "draw them in." Though some of these may be good and useful in the work, if God does not move the hearts of men, no amount of human effort will bring about the victory that God has purposed.

Nehemiah recognized this fact when he prayed in the first chapter. He prays, "O Lord, let your ear be attentive to the prayer of this your servant and to the prayer of your servants who delight in revering your name. Give your servant success today by granting him favor in the presence of this man" (Nehemiah 1:11). Nehemiah knew that if God did not grant him success, the project would fail before it began. We are going to look at three very distinct statements Nehemiah makes concerning the provision of God found in Nehemiah chapter two.

Believe in the Providence of God

"And because the gracious hand of my God was upon me, the king granted my requests." ~ Nehemiah 2:8b

How do you see the circumstances in your life? Are they coincidental or providential? For a good many people, including Christians, the world is filled with coincidental circumstances that have nothing to do with the providential workings of God. There is a sense in which many believers have closed their eyes to the activity of God and have shut their ears to the voice of Christ. Vainly they go through their lives with the notion they are on their own and though God can save them from their sins, He is relatively powerless to affect the course and condition of the world. Nothing could be farther from the truth.

Nehemiah clearly understood any favor he received from King Artaxerxes was not just circumstance or good luck; the favor Nehemiah received from the king was a direct result of the influence and providence of God. Most people would have viewed the kindness that Nehemiah received as just a coincidence or a bit of good fortune. Some might assume that Nehemiah simply caught the king in a good mood. However, Nehemiah understood, in greater depth, the reality of why he received favor from King Artaxerxes: the hand of Almighty God was with him.

Most people don't see the providential hand of God because they don't expect to. Most people don't expect to see God's activity simply because they are unaware of the leadership of God in their lives. Because of this, many Christians simply fail to seek God's provision for their activities, concluding that their lives are left to the whims of chance and circumstance. They drift about in their walk with Christ much like a leaf on the wind, without direction and without much purpose.

Understand that the gracious hand of God is upon those who are passionately following the plan of God and are willing to open their eyes to see His activity! 2 Chronicles 16:9 states, "For the eyes of the Lord range throughout the earth to strengthen those whose hearts are fully committed to him." God wants to provide everything we will ever need to carry out His will in this world. The problem lies not in the ability of God to provide for us but in our willingness to follow His leadership.

From Vision to Victory

Consider the dilemma of Moses. In Exodus chapters 2-4, God and Moses have a remarkable discussion concerning God's call in his life. For every inadequacy that Moses raised concerning his abilities, God countermanded it with His divine provision. Here is a taste of the conversation:

> Moses said to the LORD, "O Lord, I have never been eloquent, neither in the past nor since you have spoken to your servant. I am slow of speech and tongue." The LORD said to him, "Who gave man his mouth? Who makes him deaf or mute? Who gives him sight or makes him blind? Is it not I, the LORD? Now go; I will help you speak and teach you what to say." ~ Exodus 4:10-12

This grand debate between Moses and God always ends with God's promised provision for the task at hand. Even when Moses begged God to send another, God brings Aaron into the picture and gives Moses a fellow worker for the task. Our Father in Heaven is always providing for the work He has commanded. To live with that understanding gives a greater confidence in the work we're called to do.

Ephesians 2:10 reads, "For we are God's workmanship, created in Christ Jesus to do good works, which God prepared in advance for us to do." If God prepared the works for us to do, and He strongly supports those who are fully His, it stands to reason then He will provide all the resources for us to accomplish His vision.

Publicly Acknowledge the Provision of God

"I also told them about the gracious hand of my God upon me and what the king had said to me." ~ Nehemiah 2:18

There is strength in numbers. If we are to go from vision to victory, it will be hand in hand with the people of God. Nehemiah shared his passion with the people (v. 17a), he shared God's plan with the people (v. 17b), now he must share how God has provided. This is of critical importance because without this understanding, the people might begin to believe it was all because of Nehemiah's persuasiveness and skill that the work had received such a remarkable endorsement from the king. Their faith would have rested in the wrong place and on the wrong person. It is critical because all those involved in the project must have their faith firmly anchored in God.

Another reason for this is the need for unity. People need to know God is behind the project or they will quickly disperse when the going gets difficult. The fact is, there is no one called in the Kingdom of God to a life of isolation. We are meant to be servants together in this world, and when God moves upon the life of one of us, all of us should respond.

A good example of this is mountain climbing. Take four people, all with the same destination, but not all with the same function. Many people think the lead climber is the one who is of greatest importance. However, the lead climber puts his life in the hands of the other three, trusting that if he should slip, the others are anchored well enough to keep him from falling. The lead climber can climb confidently, trusting the others will hold him up. Also, no one climbs any faster than all the others. Basically, you must climb together or you don't climb at all. 2 Chronicles 30:12 speaks to this, "Also in Judah the hand of God was on the people to give them unity of mind to carry out what the king and his officials had ordered, following the word of the Lord."

Nehemiah knew he needed God's people working together in unity under the mighty hand of God so he shared with them how God had already provided. Ephesians 4:16 underscores our need for each other, "From him the whole body, joined and held together by every supporting ligament, grows and builds itself up in love, as each part does its work." The evidence of God's hand upon one of us should move all of us.

Stand Confident on the Preeminence of God

I answered them by saying, "The God of heaven will give us success" ~ Nehemiah 2:20a

When difficulty and hardship come, where do you stand? There will always be detractors in your life who will seek to disrupt the activity of God. Some may come from outside your circle of effort, trying to keep the work of God from progressing. Others might come from within, seeming partners in the project, all-the-while undermining the work with their lack of enthusiasm or down-right rebellion. It doesn't matter. If you have been given a vision from God to go forward in a task, you must carry it on to completion. God is with you and you will need to stand confident on that fact.

Nehemiah faced his first conflict and how he responded would set the course of his faithfulness throughout the remainder of this enterprise. Three men from outside the project of rebuilding the wall (Sanballat, Tobiah, and Geshem) mocked and ridiculed Nehemiah for his efforts (see: Nehemiah 2:19). However, Nehemiah never stopped. Without going into a lengthy debate or discussion with those who opposed him, he simply stated that his confidence was in the Lord.

When people come against you, what do you tell them? I was called to a small church with little resources and few people. It was a church which needed a restart. I heard from all sides that the work was too hard, the church's reputation was smeared, no one would come, God had left the work, and a host of other negative comments designed to keep me from the work. However, I knew then as I know now that God's hand is with us and that the God of heaven would give us success! I dismissed the arguments, pressed into the work with the few who were left, and God rebuilt the church.

Jehoshaphat, king of Judah, faced a difficult situation. 2 Chronicles 18:31 says, "When the chariot commanders saw Jehoshaphat, they thought, 'This is the king of Israel.' So they turned to attack him, but Jehoshaphat cried out, and the LORD helped him. God drew them away from him." Ephesians 6:10-11 states, "Finally, be strong in the Lord and in his mighty power. Put on the full armor of God so that you can take your stand against the devil's schemes." Where do you stand? If you do not stand upon the preeminence of

God, you will find that you stand on quicksand and the detractors and persecutors will overcome your willingness to continue.

If we are to go from vision to victory, it will come from the mighty hand of God. The clarity of our purpose, the cooperation of God's people, and our confidence in the face of difficulty come from knowing the mighty hand of God is with us. Remember what Gamaliel said to the Sanhedrin concerning the work of the Apostles:

> "Therefore, in the present case I advise you: Leave these men alone! Let them go! For if their purpose is of human origin, it will fail. But if it is from God, you will not be able to stop these men; you will only find yourselves fighting against God." ~ Acts 5:38-39

This is true of all who stand in the path of God's purpose. It is, ultimately, not you they're fighting, but God. He will win the day. Trust to His provision for the task before you and know it is He who will carry you from vision to victory.

Points to Ponder:

How do you see your circumstances: coincidental or providential?

Who have you told concerning God's provision in your life and work?

What do you do when difficulties or hardships come?

From Vision to Victory

Chapter Four:
The People of God

"The harvest is plentiful but the workers are few. Ask the Lord of the harvest, therefore, to send out workers into his harvest field." ~ Matthew 9:37-38

I HAVE OFTEN wondered why in the United States, with over 100 million protestant church members, our country is steadily declining spiritually, socially, and morally. How is it that the body of Christ in America is not making a greater impact in the nation around us?

Did you know if a church with fifty members each just brought one person to Jesus every year and taught each new person to do the same, then that church would have brought 51,200 people to Jesus in ten years? That is just one believer reaching one person in one year! Do you think that in 365 days you would be able to lead one person to Christ? If two would reach one person in one year, that would still be 25,600 people reached in ten years! Do you see the impact the church would have in our communities if we would rise up and take hold of the opportunities God gives us to be

Christian witnesses in a world desperate for salvation? A 2012 article from Christianity Today states:

> Although nearly three in four Christians say they feel comfortable sharing the gospel, the majority do not do so. New findings from LifeWay Research – self-described as "distressing results" – indicate that 61 percent of evangelical Christians fail to share their faith on a regular basis, even though they believe it is their responsibility to do so. Moreover, nearly half of those respondents said they have not invited a non-Christian friend to church in the past six months. However, only 21 percent of respondents said they pray every day for their non-Christian acquaintances, and 20 percent said they rarely or never pray for the spiritual status of non-Christians.[2]

Based on this national survey, only one in five Christians even pray for the lost, let alone share their faith with them. The old adage states 80 percent of the people watch while 20

[2] http://www.christianitytoday.com/gleanings/2012/august/majority-of-churchgoers-never-share-their-faith-lifeway.htm

percent of the people work. It is disturbing to think that many who belong to a church rarely do anything to support the work and most don't ever live with a kingdom perspective. The fact is, the majority of church members do nothing more than attend a Sunday morning church service.

Look around at the church today and ask yourself if you are a contributor to the cause or the solution. If the church is to rise and be an effective and powerful force for change it will require each of us. Jesus said this in Matthew 9:37-38, "The harvest is plentiful but the workers are few. Ask the Lord of the harvest, therefore, to send out workers into his harvest field." If we are to go from vision to victory it will require each of us working together in the Master's field.

In the unfolding drama of the Nehemiah Project, Nehemiah has come to the place where victory can only be won with the aid of the people of God. Nehemiah had the passion, he discovered the plan, and he has seen God's provision. The people of God must now work together to accomplish the vision God has given.

Victory will only be won together. Four things can be seen as the people of God began this good work. These four things must be a reality in our church today if we are to gain the victory.

They all had a Common Objective

When Nehemiah shared the vision and made it known that God had already provided the victory, the people of God quickly rallied to the task of rebuilding the wall. In verse 18 of chapter two they replied to Nehemiah, "Let us start rebuilding." There is nothing profound in these words, just a simple declaration that they were going to be involved in the project. Chapter three of Nehemiah is filled with the names of people who were involved. The bigger picture was understood and the people of God rallied to the task of rebuilding.

There is a principle in Scripture which states the need for unity in the church. This need for unity was one of the closing prayers of Jesus.

> My prayer is not for them alone. I pray also for those who will believe in me through their message, that all of them may be one, Father, just as you are in me and I am in you. May they also be in us so that the world may believe that you have sent me. ~ John 17:20-21

In fact, Jesus said a house divided would not stand (Mark 3:25). Look in the book of Genesis to see an example of this.

In Genesis chapter 11 we see the endeavor to build the tower of Babel. God addresses His concern in verse six. "The Lord said, 'If as one people speaking the same language they have begun to do this, then nothing they plan to do will be impossible for them.'" Though the example is a negative one in that the people were trying to do something against the will of God, the principle holds true—there is strength in having a common objective.

So what is the common objective of the people of God today? Do you even know what the objective is? This could be the reason why there is so little actual work being done for the cause of Christ compared to the wealth of people who claim allegiance to Him. Philippians 1:27 speaks to this, "Whatever happens, conduct yourselves in a manner worthy of the gospel of Christ. Then, whether I come and see you or only hear about you in my absence, I will know that you stand firm in one spirit, contending as one man for the faith of the gospel." Our objective is clear. We are to contend for the faith of the gospel. That is, we are to grow in faith as well as pass our faith out to those who need it. The problem lies in the fact that most don't live with this clear common objective in mind.

They each had a Certain Task

Not only did the people of God have a common objective, the rebuilding of the wall; they each had a certain section upon which they would begin the reconstruction. It would have been a foolish thing for them to concentrate their efforts upon only one section at a time. The majority of the people then would have been wasted since only a fraction of the workers could work on one section. So, rather than wasting their resources, they were divided up into small work parties to begin rebuilding on every section of the wall. The need was so great that there was plenty of work to go around.

It is true that many hands make light work, but too many hands are a waste of workers. In the church today, there is plenty of work to go around. There is never a time when a Christian has nothing to do in the Kingdom of God. If you find you are bored in your Christian walk and you think there is nothing to do, go back to point one and realize you may have lost sight of the objective all together. Jesus said that the harvest is plentiful! Each of us has an obligation to do what we can in the advancement of God's plan.

We have, as Christians, been gifted by the Spirit of God to function uniquely within the body of Christ, the church. We don't all have the same things to do, but we do all have something to do. Paul states this in 1 Corinthians 12:4-6, "There are different kinds of gifts, but the same Spirit. There are different kinds of service, but the same Lord. There are different kinds of working, but the same God works all of them in all men."

However, God does not want a bunch of "Lone-Ranger Christians" running around doing their own thing without consideration of the whole. So we read in 1 Corinthians 12:7, "Now to each one the manifestation of the Spirit is given for the common good." We need to continually ask ourselves, "How does this help the kingdom of God and the Body of Christ, the church?" In Nehemiah's case, the people needed to ask, "Does my section support the whole wall?" There are often too many people doing their own thing without ever thinking of the effect on the entire church. Again we read in 1 Corinthians 12:25, "So that there may be no division in the body, but that its parts should have equal concern for each other."

Some might ask, "How do I know what my part is?" Though this is not a book on spiritual discernment and giftedness, I think it is good to touch on a couple of principles. First, are you doing what you know to do? Philippians 3:16 says, "Only let us live up to what we have already attained." It is important to do the things you know to do. James 4:17 says, "Anyone, then, who knows the good he ought to do and doesn't do it, sins." Second, are you learning and growing in the Word of God? Romans 12:2 reads, "Do not conform any longer to the pattern of this world, but be transformed by the renewing of your mind. Then you will be able to test and approve what God's will is—his good, pleasing and perfect will." In order to know what God wants from you, let your mind be transformed by the Word of God. Live in a continual cycle of these two principles and you will find yourself moving forward in God's will.

They were dedicated to completing the work

In reading Nehemiah chapter 3 you cannot help but sense the drive and determination to complete the work. Fathers and children, men and women, young and old, all put their hands to the task and endeavored to do that which God had purposed for them. In fact, it is said of one man in verse 20, "Next to him, Baruch son of Zabbai zealously repaired another section, from the angle to the entrance of the house Eliashib the high priest." What a statement to make: he *zealously* worked! Can that be said of you?

In the church today there needs to be a dedication to completing the work God has given us to do. In John 4:35, Jesus told His disciples to open their eyes and see the fields that are already ripe to harvest! We need to fix our lives with a zealous determination to do the work God has given us. Lack of dedication to the work of God has left much of the work undone — or waiting on someone else to do it. Imagine if everyone left the work for someone else, no one would ever do anything. Jesus tells us to work while we still have the light (John 9:4). That is, work while you have life, for the night (death) is coming when no one can work. Galatians 6:9 states, "Let us not become weary in doing good, for at the proper time we will reap a harvest if we do not give up." I'm afraid too many have given up.

I guarantee you the devil will attempt to find a way to keep you dedicated to the things of this world rather than the things of God. God's word says men should lift up holy hands in prayer (1 Timothy 2:8), but the prayer meetings of the church are often poorly attended or altogether abandoned. Paul speaks of one of his companions in 2 Timothy 4:10, "For Demas, because he loved this world, has deserted me and has gone to Thessalonica." So often we let the cares of this world dictate the directions and determinations of our lives. There have been many in this day and age who have abandoned the church simply because they find the task of working for the Kingdom of God not instantly gratifying. Or, worse yet, they participate in the church life as long as they can continue to receive some sort of benefit without any contribution on their part. Zealous, sacrificial service is a lost reality in many, if not most, churches today.

They Willingly Cooperated with Each Other

An interesting thing takes place in Nehemiah chapter three. These people worked together. In verse five we find the men of Tekoa repairing a section, then way over in verse 27 there they are again, repairing another section. Do you know what was happening? They were cooperating with the other teams of workers so that the project would be finished in as little time as possible. They didn't just finish their own section and go home while the rest kept working—they jumped in and helped where they could. In verses four and thirty we find Meshullam son of Berekiah working. Again, in verses four and twenty-one we find Meremoth son of Uriah working. Time and again we find this cooperation to complete the work of rebuilding the wall.

Between churches we rarely see this kind of cooperation. Often churches are so segregated from one another that having true Kingdom cooperation would be a miracle. This stems from an attitude of sanctimonious separation within the congregations of God's people. It is true we do not all have the same tasks to do or load to carry, but we are meant to be headed in the same direction. We need to realize that it takes cooperation to finish the task. We cannot think we have all the necessary resources at our personal disposal to be able to accomplish the work we are called to do. There is a motto I have heard in the Southern Baptist Convention which says: "Doing together what we cannot do apart." We must work together, or eventually we might not work at all. Let's look at some key statements made about the first church of Jerusalem:

> They devoted themselves to the apostles' teaching and to the fellowship, to the breaking of bread and to prayer. All the believers were together and had everything in common. Every day they continued to meet together in the temple courts. They broke bread in their homes and ate together with glad and sincere hearts. And the Lord added to their number daily those who were being saved. ~ Acts 2:42-47

We forget the fact that we are on this journey together. And, in forgetting this, we end up working toward different objectives. We may have individual, personal, successes but without cooperation the church suffers and fractures. Paul entreats the Corinthian church in 1 Corinthians 1:10, "I appeal to you, brothers, in the name of our Lord Jesus Christ, that all of you agree with one another so that there may be no divisions among you and that you may be perfectly united in mind and thought."

Could you imagine the potential the church would have if all who belonged to Christ would work together toward the same objective? If this became the identifying mark of the churches in America, there is no height to which God could not take us. We only limit ourselves when we fail to work together in one accord for the advancement of the Kingdom of God. We don't all have the same tasks, but we should all have the same goals and be willing to work with one another, not giving up until the final trumpet sounds and our work on earth is done.

Points to Ponder:

Does everyone hold to the same vision, or are there divisions in the work?

Do you know what part you have in the plan?

Is there mutual cooperation between participants?

From Vision to Victory

Chapter Five:
Facing Persecution

"Blessed are those who are persecuted because of righteousness, for theirs is the kingdom of heaven." ~ Matthew 5:10

From Vision to Victory

ACCORDING TO A survey done by Open Doors, and reported in the Huffington Post, Christian persecution nearly doubled from the year 2012 to 2013:

> Reported cases of Christians killed for their faith around the world doubled in 2013 from the year before, with Syria accounting for more than the whole global total in 2012, according to an annual survey. Open Doors, a non-denominational group supporting persecuted Christians worldwide, said on Wednesday it had documented 2,123 "martyr" killings, compared with 1,201 in 2012. There were 1,213 such deaths in Syria alone last year, it said. "This is a very minimal count based on what has been reported

in the media and we can confirm," said Frans Veerman, head of research for Open Doors. Estimates by other Christian groups put the annual figure as high as 8,000.[3]

It seems that, in the United States, there is still a sense of safety and freedom for the Christian faith. Yet, turbulent times are on the rise, even in the land of liberty. Television shows, movies and a host of other broadcast media paint Christians as a foolish, monolithic subculture of America that does nothing more than hold back the progress and advancement of the human condition. Christian opposition to such things as gay marriage, abortion, legalized drug use and other less-than-moral changes in the culture is viewed with condescension by many who stand upon elevated platforms of social significance.

Yet, we're told by the Lord Jesus that such things would occur.

All this I have told you so that you will not go astray. They will put you out of the synagogue; in fact, a time is coming when anyone who kills you will think he is offering a service to God.

---

[3] http://www.huffingtonpost.com/2014/01/09/christian-persecution_n_4568286.html

> They will do such things because they have not
> known the Father or me. I have told you this, so
> that when the time comes you will remember
> that I warned you. I did not tell you this at first
> because I was with you. ~ John 16:1-4

In this chapter we are going to face the fact that persecution is an ongoing experience in the lives of Christians everywhere around the world, even here in the United States.

In the story of the Nehemiah Project, Nehemiah, and those who were faithful in their working to rebuild the wall of Jerusalem, found that they faced stern opposition and strong antagonists. From this story we are going to discover four truths concerning persecution. But in those truths we will find what it takes to succeed despite the opposition that we encounter.

Persecution is Real

Even from the beginning of the project, there was persecution for the people rebuilding the wall of Jerusalem. In Nehemiah 2:19 it begins with ridiculing, in 4:1 it grew to anger and incense, in 4:7-8 it grew to very angry and plotting against them, and in chapter six it climaxed at scheming to murder those who were rebuilding the wall. At every turn there was persecution against those who were faithful to God and living according to His will, especially against Nehemiah who was the visionary for the project. Those who endeavor to live for the Lord Jesus find that they are no stranger to the escalation of persecution. There is no shortage of texts in the Scriptures that speak to the reality of persecution toward those who are willingly obedient to God.

> ➤ Psalm 55:12-14: "If an enemy were insulting me, I could endure it; if a foe were raising himself against me, I could hide from him. But it is you, a man like myself, my companion, my close friend, with whom I once enjoyed sweet fellowship as we walked with the throng at the house of God."
> ➤ Matthew 5:11: "Blessed are you when people insult you, persecute you and falsely say all kinds of evil against you because of me."
> ➤ John 15:20a: "Remember the words I spoke to you: 'No servant is greater than his master.' If they persecuted me, they will persecute you also."

71

> ➤ 2Timothy 3:12: "In fact, everyone who wants to live a godly life in Christ Jesus will be persecuted."
> ➤ 1Peter 2:21: "To this you were called, because Christ suffered for you, leaving you an example, that you should follow in his steps."

The danger comes, for many, when they don't think they will or should ever have to face persecution of any kind. They blissfully go through their life, unaware of the fact there is an enemy that stands against Christ. So in order to maintain a stable life, they simply play along with the current condition of the day. In WWII, those who worked to maintain an element of friendship with the forces of evil were known as... collaborators. So James 4:4 says, "You adulterous people, don't you know that friendship with the world is hatred toward God? Anyone who chooses to be a friend of the world becomes an enemy of God."

If you are not facing any difficulty for being a Christian, it may very well be you are living a life that does not reflect the life of Christ. Now understand what persecution is. It is not the bill collector calling because you are two months late on a payment. It is not having a personality conflict with another person. Persecution is being antagonized simply because you are living out your Christian faith. I challenge you to take this week and try to live in every way to please God. Try it for a week and see what happens, and then record your findings. You may discover that there are more people around you than you think who are against Christ.

The Persecutors Fabricate a Reason

If there was one thing that was true, the persecutors of Nehemiah and the Israelites believed they had a reason for standing in opposition to the project: they hated Israel and did not want to see the establishment of Jerusalem again. The persecutors had no need for God and no desire for God's people to be back in the land doing things that looked like they were gaining strength. Nehemiah 2:10 says, "When Sanballat the Horonite and Tobiah the Ammonite official heard about this, they were very much disturbed that someone had come to promote the welfare of the Israelites." You can almost hear these men declare: "How dare they! Let's bring this to an end!" They persecuted Israel simply because they hated Israel.

Persecution happens, my friends, simply because people hate the Lord Jesus Christ – and us, vicariously. Jesus says, "If the world hates you, keep in mind that it hated me first" (John 15:18). Again He says in verse 21 of the same chapter, "They will treat you this way because of my name, for they do not know the One who sent me." Christ, and the Christian who is living to please Him, is an exposing light that reveals the hidden evils and darkness of the human heart.

If there is one thing the world would like us to do, it is to keep quiet about Jesus. And it seems, at times, there are many who would call themselves Christians who feel the same way. If you wonder about that, remember what Jesus said, "A man's enemies will be the members of his own household" (Matthew 10:36). We are living in times, today, where Christianity is the singular faith wherein persecution is tolerated in some cultures and encouraged in others. When Paul instructs Timothy to "Preach the Word," he tells him why: "For the time will come when men will not put up with sound doctrine. Instead, to suit their own desires, they will gather around them a great number of teachers to say what itching ears want to hear" (see 2 Timothy 4:1-4). The Christian faith and Christian people live as a continual reminder of the reality of God's judgment and mercy:

> But thanks be to God, who always leads us in triumphal procession in Christ and through us spreads everywhere the fragrance of the

knowledge of him. For we are to God the aroma of Christ among those who are being saved and those who are perishing. To the one we are the smell of death; to the other, the fragrance of life. And who is equal to such a task? ~ 2 Corinthians 2:14-16

Always remember: the persecution you face for living out your Christian faith is simply the expression of those who are opposed to God. But how are you to respond?

The Persecuted have a Response

In the story of Nehemiah, Nehemiah didn't retaliate or try to "take on" those who would come against him. In fact, he took no offensive posture at all. He simply trusted himself to the One who called him to the task and who would protect him in the strife. What did Nehemiah do? He prayed:

Hear us, O our God, for we are despised. Turn their insults back on their own heads. Give them over as plunder in a land of captivity. Do not cover up their guilt or blot out their sins from your sight, for they have thrown insults in the face of the builders. ~ Nehemiah 4:4-5

So often when we are persecuted, we tend to strike back and attack those who come against us. We are like Peter in the garden (John 18:10-11). When he saw the soldiers come against Jesus, he drew his sword and began hacking away at the nearest "bad guy" he could find. The Scriptures, however, give us four responses we must have in order to gain victory in the face of persecution, and none of them are to attack the persecutors.

First, you must: *Pray*. Matthew 5:44: "But I tell you: Love your enemies and pray for those who persecute you." This act of devotion to God is an indication of your relationship with Him. Can you pray for your enemies? You must if you want to respond to persecution in a way that is harmonious to your Christian faith.

Next, you must be: *Patient*. Romans 12:12: "Be joyful in hope, patient I affliction, faithful in prayer." How long are you willing to endure? Can you be patient in affliction? The first response to persecution is to fight or flee, but enduring patience is a mark of deep faith.

Then, you must: *Persevere*. Hebrews 10:36: "You need to persevere so that when you have done the will of God, you will receive what he has promised." Keep pressing on in the work God has given you to do. Those detractors are doing what they do in order to keep you from finishing the work, tripping you up, and preventing the will of God to be accomplished. You, however, must continue faithfully in the task that God commands.

Finally, you must: *Praise.* 1 Peter 4:16: "However, if you suffer as a Christian, do not be ashamed, but praise God that you bear that name." Perhaps the most challenging of the four, being able to praise in the midst of persecution is hard. But be reminded you are shining the light of Christ, testifying to His great power and love, and identifying completely with Him. Being persecuted for your faith marks you as one who walks with Christ.

These four responses to persecution are the Biblical method for every Christian. If you find yourself acting in this manner when persecution comes, you will find that there is ample strength to endure and succeed in the face of suffering.

The Persecutors receive the Repercussions

Ultimately the persecutors are persecuting God. I believe Nehemiah knew this and we see it in his prayer as he prayed for those who would come against the builders of the wall (see Nehemiah 4:4-5). He prayed that the destruction the persecutors had plotted against the builders would come upon their own heads.

77

From Vision to Victory

Sometimes we wonder why it seems that evil prospers and wickedness goes unpunished. Jeremiah the prophet wondered the same in Jeremiah 12:1, "Why does the way of the wicked prosper? Why do all the faithless live at ease?" Such questions might be asked today. Yet, the Psalmist says this:

> When I tried to understand all this, it was oppressive to me till I entered the sanctuary of God; then I understood their final destiny. Surely you place them on slippery ground; you cast them down to ruin. How suddenly they are destroyed, completely swept away by terrors! As a dream when one awakens, so when you arise, O Lord, you will despise them as fantasies. ~ Psalm 73:16-20

What is essential to realize is this: God will bring to bear upon the head of everyone the just reward for their actions, whether good or evil. Just because the world has grown hazardous for Christians and persecution is real, don't despair. There will be a day of reckoning. 2 Thessalonians 1:6 says, "God is just: He will pay back trouble to those who trouble you." Those who come against the people of God will have God to answer to on the day of final judgment.

We may have inequity now, for the little while that we are in this world, but God will avenge Himself and His people upon those who mistreated them. Hebrews 10:30-31: "For we know him who said, 'It is mine to avenge; I will repay,' and again, 'the Lord will judge his people.' It is a dreadful thing to fall into the hands of the living God."

It may seem unfair that Christians are so painfully treated today. But there is coming a day when the wrath of God will be revealed against all ungodliness and wickedness of men. There is coming a day when God will right every wrong, set straight the crooked, and avenge Himself on those who have persecuted Him in persecuting His people. That day is coming and there is nothing anyone can do to stop it. So the question is: what side of God's wrath will you be on? Will you receive His wrath or be avenged by it?

My friends, persecution against the people of God is real. No matter how we try and explain to them that what they do is wrong, those who persecute still think they have a valid reason to attack Christians. Whatever their reasoning is, our response must be one that brings glory to God. And no matter how bad it gets, remember there will be a day that brings equity for those who were faithful to the end.

Points to Ponder:

How have you found yourself persecuted?

Are you willing to let God deal with the persecutors and not take matters into your own hands?

What response will you give those who persecute you?

Chapter Six:
Embracing Perseverance

"Perseverance must finish its work so that you may be mature and complete, not lacking anything." ~ James 1:4

From Vision to Victory

WHEN YOU CONSIDER success, what images come to mind? Most people consider success to be an event in a person's life. That is, they will say something like, "I have finally become successful." What they mean is they have achieved a particular goal or objective for their life. However, in the Christian's life, it seems we view success in a different light. Many seem to think, and I judge this by the behavior I see, that success in the Kingdom of God is simply maintaining and getting by. For some, it seems, their attitude is: "If we can just muddle through this life without causing too much of an uproar then we have been successful as a Christian."

But I think many Christians truly do want to see the Kingdom of Christ grow and impact the community and the culture. They wish there was more being done, but wishing for something is little more than hollow lip-service. In fact, and I've said this many times, the difference between wishing for something and wanting something is the willingness to pay the price. It costs something to gain victory – sacrifice and service, perseverance and pain. Towns recover from tornadoes not because people simply wished the storm never happened, but because they embraced the demand for effort and put their hands to the work... and worked until they were done.

Success in the Kingdom of God is not just about survival but total victory. However, total victory will not be won without determination. It takes perseverance and endurance for us to experience the victory that is ours in Christ. Do you believe that victory is yours? Then, to experience that victory, you must be willing to pursue it with all your heart. In this chapter we are going to see what it takes for us to find victory in our lives—what it takes to persevere.

We must maintain an Awareness of Total Victory

Nehemiah 4:6 says, "So we rebuilt the wall till all of it reached half its height, for the people worked with all their heart." At this point in their work they had achieved a great deal. They had rebuilt the wall until it had reached half its height. Many would have just stopped at this point and reveled in the achievement. Some may have even said, "Isn't this enough? Haven't we done enough for this project?" In the effort to rebuild the wall of Jerusalem, there was no question in the minds of the builders of what total victory must look like. The only thing that would be right would be the full restoration of the wall of Jerusalem. It was all or nothing!

Is this the attitude in your Christian walk? Are you aware of what total victory looks like? If God has given you a vision and clear direction from His word, are you willing to see it through to the end? Though I only speak anecdotally about this, I have heard the average tenure of a pastor in a church is roughly 18 months. If that is the case, I wonder just how much perseverance there is. As I write this, I live in a town where two of the churches have pastors who have been at their positions more than 30 years! They are respected and highly regarded in the community for they have proved themselves in endurance.

Yet, for many Christians, the idea of staying with a project and working at it with all their heart is tantamount to lunacy. For them, the Christian life is about the moment – living for the exuberant and ecstatic experience they call an encounter with God. We have reduced the Christian life to little more than an emotional church experience. And, in so doing, have abandoned one of the predominant characteristics of the Christian faith – perseverance. Consider what is said in James 1:4: "Perseverance must finish its work so that you may be mature and complete, not lacking anything." Paul recognizes the need for perseverance in Galatians 6:9, "Let us not become weary in doing good, for at the proper time we will reap a harvest if we do not give up."

We must quit being satisfied with the shallow and superficial. It is time for churches across America and around the world to recognize the high calling we have in Christ and to live our lives with the knowledge that only through perseverance will victory be attained. So, let me ask you, where do you need to gain a vision of victory in your life? Do you need to recapture this mentality: only through endurance will the race be won? Real victory only comes to those who are aware of the need for perseverance. We need to have an awareness of victory in every facet of our life. You will never be able to persevere in your Christian walk until you can see that victory is yours, and it is within your reach.

We must live with the Attitude of Complete Success

The people worked at it with all their heart! Victory, success, whatever you want to call it, is only won when we are willing to dive in with our entire lives. The builders of the wall were determined to carry out the project God had called them to with their whole heart. In fact, it was because of their determination they were able to complete the entire project in less than two months! Consider that! They rebuilt an entire wall around the city of Jerusalem in less than two months, and most churches have difficulty just getting nursery workers.

What is the attitude of your life concerning the victory that could be yours in Christ? Do you work with all your heart on those things God has called you to? Any success in any field requires a complete commitment of your life! As I'm writing this, the Super Bowl has just been played and the Seattle Seahawks came away victorious. It was a stellar achievement, accomplished by skillful players, knowledgeable coaches and raucous fans! However, there was something else they had – they had heart.

But that is always the case for the truly victorious. Football teams don't train to just get into the playoffs but to win the Super Bowl. Professional golf players don't hope to come away in the top 50 at Augusta but to win the Masters. Baseball teams don't try and go even on the season but to win the World Series. Do you fight in your Christian life to become everything God has called you to? If all you do in your Christian life is striving to just get by, you will get nowhere. If you possess an attitude for complete success, you will find your life in Christ propelled to great and wonderful heights. The Bible speaks clearly about the attitude of perseverance:

➢ Matthew 11:12: "From the days of John the Baptist until now, the kingdom of heaven has been forcefully advancing, and forceful men lay hold of it." Do you have the mindset to grab hold of God's kingdom and His purpose with force?
➢ Luke 13:24: "Make every effort to enter through the narrow door, because many, I tell you, will try to enter and will not be able to." Are you making every effort to enter in the narrow door?
➢ 1 Corinthians 9:24: "Do you not know that in a race all the runners run, but only one gets the prize? Run in such a way as to get the prize." Do you run the race of life with the singular goal of total victory?

> ➤ Philippians 2:12: "Therefore, my dear friends...continue to work out your salvation with fear and trembling." Are you "working out" what God has worked in?
> ➤ Philippians 3:14: "I press on toward the goal to win the prize for which God has called me heavenward in Christ Jesus." Do you press on toward the goal to win the prize?
> ➤ 2 Timothy 1:6: "For this reason I remind you to fan into flame the gift of God, which is in you through the laying on of my hands." Are you fanning into flame God's gift in your life?

My friends, you have got to believe that if you pursue God's purpose and vision with your whole heart then God will honor your efforts and give you great success. Again, don't think of it in terms of worldly successes. God's victories are Kingdom victories – and you must make sure you keep such a mindset. If you only live for the shallow, worldly and temporary successes of this life, you have missed the greatest triumphs.

One major problem currently plaguing the church is a laziness and indifference when it comes to our spiritual lives. We think we're alright so we think God thinks we're alright, so we don't expend much effort at all when it comes to our life in Christ. For us to be able to persevere in this walk with Christ, we must believe the whole-hearted pursuit of God's great purposes will result in success.

For an aircraft, the "attitude" of the aircraft determines if it is pointing up or down. A plane with a "positive attitude" is one with its nose pointed toward the sky – a "negative attitude" means it is pointing toward the ground. Now, based upon my limited understanding, the attitude of the aircraft determines if it will gain or lose altitude. How much more true in our spiritual striving is the need to have the right attitude! Our attitude toward Christ and His calling in our life will determine the altitude of our victories.

Antagonists must not cause Discouragement

The builders of the wall were plagued with a continual barrage of negativity from their antagonists. Though it did disturb them, it didn't deter them from their efforts to rebuild the wall. Nehemiah continued to press them into the reality that it was God who called them to the task and God would strengthen their hands for the work. As they struggled to rebuild, they were directly threatened by their antagonists:

From Vision to Victory

> Also our enemies said, "Before they know it or
> see us, we will be right there among them and
> will kill them and put an end to their work."
> Then the Jews who lived near them came and
> told us ten times over, "Wherever you turn, they
> will attack us." ~ Nehemiah 4:11-12

Knowing this threat, and taking it seriously, Nehemiah did what was necessary to alleviate the danger without stopping the progress of the work. "Therefore I stationed some of the people behind the lowest points of the wall at the exposed places, posting them by families, with their swords, spears and bows" (Nehemiah 4:13). Where discouragement and fear could have destroyed the work, the people were strengthened and encouraged to continue the task God had given them (see Nehemiah 4:14-15).

For us to persevere, we need to be able to overcome the discouragement those who oppose us would have us embrace. We will be harassed, ridiculed, made fun of, threatened, laughed at, and persecuted simply because we are pursuing a vital and active relationship with Christ (again, see 2 Timothy 3:12). Many today will allow the antagonists to determine their Christian walk. That is, they will quiet their voice, calm down their activity, and down play their relationship to Jesus just to get along with those around them. How do you face the antagonism that people level against you for being a believer in Christ? If you say there is no antagonism, then ask yourself this question: Do people even know you are a Christian? The Word of God gives us some counsel on dealing with the antagonists:

➢ Nehemiah 4:14: "After I looked things over, I stood up and said to the nobles, the officials and the rest of the people, 'Don't be afraid of them. Remember the Lord, who is great and awesome, and fight for your brothers, your sons and your daughters, your wives and your homes.'" When harassed, do you remember the Lord?

➢ Psalm 34:7: "The angel of the Lord encamps around those who fear him, and he delivers them." Do you believe God surrounds you with His protection?

➢ 2 Corinthians 4:1: "Therefore, since through God's mercy we have this ministry, we do not lose heart." Are you encouraged, knowing it was God who gave you this ministry?

➢ 2 Corinthians 4:16: "Therefore we do not lose heart. Though outwardly we are wasting away, yet inwardly we are being renewed day by day." Do you find yourself renewed day by day?

➤ 1 Timothy 4:12: "Don't let anyone look down on you because you are young, but set an example for the believers in speech, in life, in love, in faith and in purity." Will you set an example for those in your life – even those who look down on you?

➤ 1 Peter 1:7: "These have come so that our faith – of greater worth than gold, which perishes even though refined by fire – may be proved genuine and may result in praise, glory and honor when Jesus Christ is revealed." Do you praise God for the opportunity to prove your faith is genuine when persecution and difficulties arise?

Just because we must deal with the antagonists who surround us, there is no reason to lose heart. If we become easily discouraged because people oppose us, we will lose the drive and desire to persevere. God expects us to press on even in the face of suffering, let alone in the midst of antagonists. We need to remember the words in 1 John 4:4, "You, dear children, are from God and have overcome them, because the one who is in you is greater than the one who is in the world." If we believe in and belong to Jesus, we have all the resources of God to overcome the enemy who will oppose us.

From Vision to Victory

It is time for us as Christians to take the battle for the souls of men back to the front lines of the war. We must be willing to persevere, and to do so no matter what the opposition would throw at us. Realize there is a victory for those who are in Christ and that victory must be a driving force in our lives. It is that victory which waits before us and should give us the motivation to persevere. To reach the victory that is ours in Christ, we must maintain an attitude of success. We cannot fail when we walk by faith in Jesus Christ.

No matter how hard it becomes and how challenging the way, if we persevere then we will succeed. If, however, we shrink back simply because the people of the world oppose us, we will fail. God expects us to continue to press the battle to the enemy's camp. Don't give up, for at the proper time you will receive the reward for you perseverance.

Points to Ponder:

What does victory look like?

What does it mean to "work with all your heart?"

How do you face antagonism?

From Vision to Victory

Chapter Seven:
The Right Priorities

"Dear friends, although I was very eager to write to you about the salvation we share, I felt I had to write and urge you to contend for the faith that was once for all entrusted to the saints." ~ Jude 1:3

AS WE COME to this chapter and look upon the project of Nehemiah, we see a group of people who seemed to have either forgotten or never truly understood why they were there. The vision was lost on them since they could not see beyond their own personal goals and expectations and dreams and desires. Basically, they would not see past themselves to live a life beyond their own selfishness.

During the campaign to build the walls of Jerusalem, many of the nobles and officials took the opportunity to make a profit off of the needs of the people. They saw the project not as a means to serve God but as a chance for their own personal growth and expansion of power and wealth. They saw no farther than the casting of their own shadows. The nobles saw this as an opportunity to take the advantage of the misfortune of those who were building the wall.

From Vision to Victory

Remember, the nobles didn't even lend a hand in the reconstruction (see Nehemiah 3:5). Consider what took place:

> Still others were saying, "We have had to borrow money to pay the king's tax on our fields and vineyards. Although we are of the same flesh and blood as our countrymen and though our sons are as good as theirs, yet we have to subject our sons and daughters to slavery. Some of our daughters have already been enslaved, but we are powerless, because our fields and our vineyards belong to others." ~ Nehemiah 5:4-5

Nehemiah responded to the nobles for this outrage:

> So I continued, "What you are doing is not right. Shouldn't you walk in the fear of our God to avoid the reproach of our Gentile enemies? I and my brothers and my men are also lending the people money and grain. But let the exacting of usury stop! Give back to them immediately their fields, vineyards, olive groves and houses, and also the usury you are charging them—the

hundredth part of the money, grain, new wine
and oil." ~ Nehemiah 5:9-11

These nobles must have taken their cue from the selfish-
sinner's book of success. You have heard of this book, no
doubt. Many famous quotes come from it: "Get while the
getting is good," "Strike while the iron is hot," and perhaps
my all-time favorite, "Look out for number one." But before
you think we have come beyond such petty selfishness, take
a look around you. The majority of the choices we make in
our lives have very little to do with living a life beyond
ourselves. Let us consider the reaction of Nehemiah and
allow God to remind us about the priority of living beyond
ourselves.

The Result of Human Reasoning

You don't have to look far to see the reality of human
reasoning in the church today. Many churches are built on
the foundation of human wisdom and understanding. Do
you realize that the church in America is now placing
billions of dollars a year into the coffers of the world just on
debt? According to Dave Ramsey, the church of America is

33 billion dollars in debt.[4] We build lavish structures and grand cathedrals to encapsulate our marvelous ability to grow a great organization. Pastors have become CEO's rather than shepherds. Deacons are board members rather than servants. Committees rule the church rather than Jesus through Spirit led believers. And the budget, rather than the Bible, determines the ministry.

Greater than this, and beyond the corporate climate of the church, is the human reasoning by which individual church members live. They come in on Sunday looking very spiritual and go out on Monday looking just like everyone else in the world. Don't think that pastors are immune. Have a pastor invited to a small church with little resources and a low budget, and that same pastor will consider such a church a mere "stepping-stone" to bigger and better things. Even I struggled with such a mindset early in ministry. No one should ever assume their own quest for greatness is the voice of God calling them. Personal ambition is rarely collaborative with God's priorities. Striving for self-importance is not God's vision for mankind and will not bring about the victorious life God has designed for those who believe.

---

[4] http://www.daveramsey.com/article/what-could-the-church-do-debt-free/lifeandmoney_church/

But what is the result of human reasoning? Simple, the result of human reasoning is stated by Nehemiah, "What you are doing is not right." Human reasoning will always lead us to do the wrong thing. The results of human reasoning are hurt and anguish for those around you and embarrassment and shame for those who live according to it. The examples found in the Scriptures are quite illustrative: The people rebuilding the wall were being sold into slavery (see Nehemiah 5:5). It was human reasoning that ended up killing Uriah (see 2 Samuel 11:14-15). Human reasoning sold Jesus for thirty pieces of silver (see Matthew 26:14-16). Human reasoning plunged the entire human race into the darkness and despair of sin (see Genesis 3:6).

Now, have you ever wondered just exactly what it is you are doing when you are living according to your own wisdom and not according to God's? Proverbs 14:12 says, "There is a way that seems right to a man, but in the end it leads to death." We so often try and justify our decisions and say that this is the best we can do. Or we use that old adage, "I'm only human." NO! If you are a born-again Christian you have passed the place where you are "only human." Ephesians 4:17 says, "So I tell you this, and insist on it in the Lord, that you must no longer live as the Gentiles do, in the futility of their thinking." If we are to gain victory and live a life beyond ourselves, we must no longer live in the futility of human wisdom.

The Requirements for Godly Living

Now we come to it! This is what it takes to live a life beyond ourselves—we need to know, and then live by, the requirements for Godly living. Nehemiah told the nobles and officials, "Shouldn't you walk in the fear of our God...?" Let me give you a bit of a definition: To *walk* in something is to live your life and conform your activities to a certain set of parameters. Now what parameters did Nehemiah set for the nobles and officials, and is also set for us? The parameter is the fear of God. To live your life in the fear of God is to live according to His very nature and character. God has established the requirements for life and if we are to fear Him, we are going to have to live according to His requirements and not our own.

We need to examine our life's priorities in light of the requirements of God and the revelation of Jesus. The book of James gives great illumination to this:

> Do not merely listen to the word, and so deceive yourselves. Do what it says. Anyone who listens to the word but does not do what it says is like a

man who looks at his face in a mirror and, after looking at himself, goes away and immediately forgets what he looks like. But the man who looks intently into the perfect law that gives freedom, and continues to do this, not forgetting what he has heard, but doing it—he will be blessed in what he does. ~ James 1:22-25

How many times have you gone to the mirror to see all the marks of time? And there, in front of the mirror, you worked to correct the aberrations and clean up the presentation before you stepped into the world for all to see. Yet, multitudes of Christians will look at the word of God and, walking away, forget what they just read and fail to put it into practice, leaving them in the same mess as when they first read it.

More often than not we walk in the light of our own counsel under the guidance of humanistic wisdom. We live within ourselves, and thus will do what we do simply because it is pleasing or beneficial to us. However, to live beyond yourselves is to live with a different set of priorities. It is to live with priorities that are focused on God and others.

Would you believe Jesus lived perfectly within the requirements of God the Father? You had better! Examine the life of Jesus and you will see His priorities were always focused outward — the relationship to His Father, and the relationship to others. Consider these statements He made: "I have come that they might have life" (John 10:10), "For even the Son of Man did not come to be served, but to serve, and to give his life as a ransom for many" (Mark 10:45), "For the Son of Man came to seek and to save what was lost" (Luke 19:10), "Father, glorify your name" (John 12:28).

Ask yourself what statement your life is making. Everything you do is a statement of what you believe and what you have determined to be a priority. Where is your focus? Are you living within yourself or beyond yourself? I hope you can say with the Apostle Paul in Romans 14:7-8, "For none of us lives to himself alone and none of us dies to himself alone. If we live, we live to the Lord; and if we die, we die to the Lord. So, whether we live or die, we belong to the Lord." Living with the right priorities is to live a life abandoned to God.

The Response from Worldly Onlookers

Do you realize that the world around you is watching to see what kind of Christian you are and thus what kind of God you claim to serve? So often we are much like the nobles and officials of the days of Nehemiah, bringing the reproach of the enemies of God upon us. So often we live within ourselves, by our own wisdom, and not by faith thus nullifying the opportunity in our lives for God to bless us and bring glory to His name. The nobles and officials at the rebuilding of the wall were bringing the reproach of their enemies since they were doing exactly what the enemies would have done anyway. Simply stated, the enemies of God were laughing at God's people. The people of God were defeating themselves without any help from the enemy at all.

Have you ever heard this statement, "I don't go to church because there are too many hypocrites there?" I can't begin to tell you how many times I have heard that very excuse from a person during a time when I was sharing Christ with them. Do you know what they are saying? "I have seen those Christians, and if that is how they behave, no thanks!" God help the lost person who may just happen to wander into a church when they're having a business meeting!

We say we believe that in Christ there is full forgiveness and redemption of the lost. We say we have the fullness of joy and the peace that passes all understanding. We say we have a changed life and a different set of priorities. We say we follow a God who loves and provides for those who trust Him. We say the Bible is the true and complete Word from God to men. We say a lot of things, but how do we live?

The world is watching, and what they see is a divorce rate equal to their own. Here's a statement from the Barna research group: "In fact, when evangelicals and non-evangelical born again Christians are combined into an aggregate class of born again adults, their divorce figure is statistically identical to that of non-born again adults: 32% versus 33%, respectively."[5]

What the world sees are a people in the church, living in bitterness and turmoil. What they see is a fractured people with a multitude of names from Assembly of God to Zion Baptist. What they see is a people who know little and trust less the promises of God. What they see is a people who know more lines from television commercials than lines from the holy Word of God. What they see are a people who know more about their favorite sports figure than about the Savior of mankind.

It is so important that we look at the entirety of our lives. It falls hard on many believers that they have a responsibility to be a light and a witness to the world – not just in words, but in actions. Have you ever thought that the way the lost looks at you is the view they have of Jesus? Are

[5] https://www.barna.org/barna-update/article/15-familykids/42-new-marriage-and-divorce-statistics-released

you depicting for the world around you what Jesus truly looks like? Ask yourself this: would Jesus do what you do? For me, there have been many things the Lord has convicted me of even as I write this chapter. So, if you think this is written just to make you feel guilty, take heart that it made me feel guilty first.

The world will respond to your activity in Christ. Your activity will either bring reproach to the name of Jesus, or respect for the name of Jesus. Matthew 5:14-16 reads, "You are the light of the world. A city on a hill cannot be hidden. Neither do people light a lamp and put it under a bowl. Instead they put it on its stand, and it gives light to everyone in the house. In the same way, let you light shine before men, that they may see your good deeds and praise your Father in heaven." You may be the only illumination of Jesus that someone else will see.

Are you ready to live a life beyond yourself? Do you understand this is the life that you are called to in Jesus Christ? If you are ready to live a life beyond yourself, then now is the time. There are some steps you can take.

First, you must abandon any notion that the world's wisdom will help you to live a right life. Proverbs 3:5-6 states, "Trust in the Lord with all your heart and lean not on your own understanding; in all your ways acknowledge him, and he will make your paths straight."

Second, you must adopt the mind of Christ in all of your activities. Romans 12:2 reads, "Do not conform any longer to the pattern of this world, but be transformed by the renewing of your mind. Then you will be able to test and approve what God's will is — his good, pleasing and perfect will." Third, you must become aware that the world is watching you in order to get a view of Jesus. Titus 2:7-8 states, "In everything set them an example by doing what is good. In your teaching show integrity, seriousness and soundness of speech that cannot be condemned, so that those who oppose you may be ashamed because they have nothing bad to say about us."

If we are to go from vision to victory, it will be only when we have abandoned self and embraced the fullness of Christ in us. We must live our lives beyond ourselves.

Points to Ponder:

What is the result of human reasoning?

What are the requirements for Godly living?

Do your words and your actions work together to verify or deny your faith in the Lord Jesus Christ?

From Vision to Victory

Chapter Eight:
A Clear Perspective

"You hypocrite, first take the plank out of your own eye, and then you will see clearly to remove the speck from your brother's eye." ~ Matthew 7:5

From Vision to Victory

ON A COLD and foggy autumn morning, we were traveling on a ferryboat from the island that we lived on to the mainland. The ferryboat captain, an old and seasoned veteran of many journeys across Puget Sound, set out from the dock and began the twenty-minute trip to the other side. Most of us were students going to school and had little awareness of the impending situation looming ahead of us. For, little did we know, the boat we were on lacked one piece of working equipment to insure a safe passage from the island to the mainland. It lacked radar. Oh, the device was there. But for some reason which remains shrouded in mystery, it broke down during the beginning of the trip.

The captain, wise in his knowledge of the area, endeavored to bring the boat safely to the mainland harbor, but the fog was so thick, there was no real means of navigation. Thirty minutes into the trip we briefly ran aground. We were lost and the only hope we had was for the fog to lift so we could finally see clearly our way to the mainland dock. The captain gingerly maneuvered the boat from the shore and we sailed around for two hours until the fog lifted and we could make our way to our original destination.

Many of us find that our Christian life is much like that boat trip I just described. We know where the destination is. We know where we are going. But a fog of confusion settles in on our life and we lose track of the direction we are going. We fail to gain victory only because we can no longer see to navigate our Christian lives. Distractions abound and we are often overcome with a sense of misdirection and confusion causing us to lose our way.

However, God has called us to live a life of clarity and certainty when it comes to knowing and following Him. No, we don't see the end from the beginning, but God gives us enough light and knowledge to keep the right course. Even as Psalm 119:105 states, "Your word is a lamp to my feet and a light for my path." Or, as 2 Peter 1:19 says, "As we have the word of the prophets made more certain, and you will do well to pay attention to it, as to a light shining in a dark place, until the day dawns and the morning star rises in your hearts."

Moreover, my friends, false guides abound. Our great danger comes when we begin to listen to the directions of these deceitful leaders. That is when we lose our way. You must realize the enemy of God is known as the great deceiver for a reason, masquerading as an angel of light (see 2 Corinthians 11:13-15). He endeavors to trick you, tempt you and ultimately take you from the true path God has placed before you. If he (the enemy) can keep us confused, off balance and ignorant of the way of life, then we have already lost. If we are to go from vision to victory, we must know how to maintain a clear perspective in the midst of confusion.

Recognize the Source

As Nehemiah was closing in on accomplishing the goal of rebuilding the wall, there was greater and stronger opposition to the final effort. One of the strategies of the opposition was to try and confuse the issue of rebuilding the wall. First they tried to trick Nehemiah into leaving the project to attend a meeting about thirty miles away in a village on the plain of Ono: "Sanballat and Geshem sent me this message: 'Come, let us meet together in one of the villages on the plain of Ono.' But they were scheming to harm me" (Nehemiah 6:2). For your information, the word

"Ono" means "grief." If Nehemiah attended their little "conference" then there would have been much grief!

They tried to confuse the issue by flat-out lying about the project and Nehemiah's role in the work. Sanballat sent a letter that read in part, "It is reported among the nations — and Geshem says it is true — that you and the Jews are plotting to revolt, and therefore you are building the wall" (Nehemiah 6:6).

Then some came with supposedly good intentions (and bad ideas) to try and get Nehemiah to sin against God (see Nehemiah 6:10-13). Nehemiah recognized this as we read in verse 13, "He [Shemaiah] had been hired to intimidate me so that I would commit a sin by doing this, and then they would give me a bad name to discredit me." Generally, they were trying to confuse the issue. They were trying to keep Nehemiah off balance so that the project would not be completed.

If we fail to recognize the source of the confusion, we run the risk of being destroyed by it. The enemy of God, and of God's people, does not want you to remain faithful to God's purpose. He will attempt to confuse, control, intimidate and lie. He will bring up past failures or surround you with naysayers. All of this is in the effort to stop the project from going forward. Even as I write this, at my church we are launching into a time of outreach and discipleship we believe is of God. It didn't take long before the attacks commenced from outside our congregation, with voices of denigration and accusation, in an attempt to keep people from participating in our fellowship.

Remember, confusion is not of God. 1 Corinthians 14:33 reads, "For God is not a God of disorder, but of peace." If we are thrown into confusion, it's not God's fault. God wants us to have clarity! So, what is the source of confusion? Well, in Nehemiah there were two sources. The first was the enemies around him.

There will always be those who will oppose you and want to keep you from doing the will of God. Some may come in and try to convince you that what you're doing is not right. Some will try and intimidate you. By various means and tactics, they will try and keep you unbalanced and off track.

The second source of confusion was the "friends" near him. In fact, it was some of the so-called prophets who tried to arrange Nehemiah's fall. Consider the purpose of our Lord Jesus. He knew His destiny was the cross, to pay the price for the sins of all mankind. However, He had a friend named Peter, who, with all good intentions, tried to prevent that eventuality (see Matthew 16:21-22). Jesus response: "Get behind me, Satan! You are a stumbling block to me; you do not have in mind the things of God, but the things of men" (Matthew 16:23).

Sometimes, even the best-intentioned people will come up with the wrong idea in trying to cope with a situation in the life of their friend. It's called bad advice and most of us have shared it without realizing. If we are going to overcome the confusion in our life, we must first recognize the source of that confusion.

So, what are the areas of confusion in your life? What has become such a stumbling block or a wall that has kept you from doing what God wants you to do? Where is it you lost "radar contact" with the destination and now you feel as if you are adrift in an open sea with no hope and no end in sight? If you have an area in your life where you find there is no clarity, only confusion, then you need to know that you have lost contact with God in that area. God is not the author of confusion—He is the God of order. Once you have recognized the source of confusion then you are able to go to the next step, which is to remember the truth.

Remember the Truth

One of the great strengths of Nehemiah was he knew exactly what God had called him to do, and there was no amount of deception or persuasion that would veer him off track. Look at the reply he sent Sanballat in Nehemiah 6:8. "I sent him this reply: 'Nothing like what you are saying is happening; you are just making it up out of your head.'" Even at the home of his friend, when a so-called prophet encouraged him to go into the temple and hide, Nehemiah knew God did not send this prophet (see Nehemiah 6:12).

There are only two things we have the opportunity to believe: the truth or a lie. From the very beginning with Adam and Eve, they had only two things to believe: God's truth or the Devil's lie. Consider the words of the serpent in the garden: "Did God really say..." (Genesis 3:1). That is the same question which rises in the thoughts of multitudes who do not know the difference between the truth and a lie. In our modern society, the Bible has been maligned and misrepresented in order to discredit those who strive to follow it.

Our confusion comes when we begin to entertain the lies as potential truth. That is, we think what we are hearing is good and pleasing and so we begin to adopt it as our belief. For example, God says, "I hate divorce" (Malachi 2:16). However, two Christians find that they have personal challenges getting along as a married couple and go to a marriage counselor. This marriage counselor tells them that divorce is a viable option so they begin to believe maybe

God was a little harsh in His judgment about divorce and, thus, they throw their lives into confusion.

If you adopt a life of continually believing a lie, you will continually live in a state of perpetual confusion. But there is hope! Jesus says, "If you hold to my teaching, you are really my disciples. Then you will know the truth, and the truth will set you free" (John 8:31-32). But, the truth will only set us free when we know it and live it.

So, let's go back to those areas of confusion in your life. What does God say about it? Are you confused in your finances? God has something to say about that. Are you confused in your relationships? God will give you some truth for that. Are you confused about your future? God holds the future in His hands. Are you confused on how to raise your children? God knows how to guide you in that area. The only thing we need is the knowledge of and willingness to abide by the truth.

We are so eager to hear all the world's philosophies and ideas, but what does God say? As the book of James says, "Do not merely listen to the word, and so deceive yourselves. Do what it says" (James 1:22). Or, be like the wise man of Matthew 7:24, building your life upon obedience to the solid rock of God's word.

Respond by Faith

How did Nehemiah respond by faith? First, he continued in the work. Simply because there were those who tried to confuse the situation and were attempting to draw Nehemiah away from the purpose that God had established didn't keep Nehemiah from continuing in the work. Faith, if it is real faith, works. Nehemiah knew what it was God had called him to do, and he stayed true to the task. Second, Nehemiah stood his ground in the face of impending disaster. The threats to his life were real. It would have been a reasonable action to take to the safety of the temple, but Nehemiah knew the work was more important than his safety. He also understood that God was true to His word and would keep Nehemiah under His divine protection.

To maintain clarity in the midst of confusion, we need to respond to the word of God by faith. The fact is, and this may seem simplistic, but the word of God is completely useless unless we put it into practice. How can we say we have faith and not live according to the word God has given us? We say we believe, but what is it that we believe? Our Christian life is lived in continual confusion when we fail to take God at His word and live according to it.

James asked the question in James 2:14, "What good is it, by brothers, if a man claims to have faith but has no deeds? Can such a faith save him?" Hebrews chapter 11 is considered by many as the great "roll-call" of faith. In each verse that begins with the statement, "by faith," there is a corresponding action or activity. And how does heaven view such people who live by faith? "The world was not worthy of them" (Hebrews 11:38).

As we saw earlier, Jesus says those who build their lives on obedience to the word of God are like a wise man who builds on a solid rock foundation (see Matthew 7:24). When the storms of confusion come they are secure because their life is built on obedience to the word of God.

Let's go back to those areas of personal challenge. Where are you confused? What does God's word say about that particular area of life? How can you respond by faith? What is God telling you to do? Is there an area of repentance you need to deal with? How about the need for forgiveness or the need to forgive another? What response does God's word tell you to do? This is where the "rubber meets the road" as it were. This is where we truly discover our relationship with Jesus and find out where He is calling us to grow. God wants us to be willing and able to stand firm in His word and for His purpose.

There are plenty of opportunities for us to remain confused in our Christian life. The sources of confusion are broad and varied and are continually present in our life. The question is, when those sources of confusion come in are we going to run back to the word of God, the source of truth, or are we going to entertain those things which cause us confusion? When we come to understand what the truth is, are we going to respond by faith in obedience or are we going to ignore what God clearly tells us? If you want to develop and maintain a clear perspective, even in the midst of confusion, it will require you to do those things which provide it.

Points to Ponder:

What people or circumstances have thrown you into confusion?

What does God's word say concerning the issues that arise in your life and work?

How can you respond by faith?

Chapter Nine:
The Thread of Prayer

"If my people, who are called by my name, will humble themselves and pray and seek my face and turn from their wicked ways, then will I hear from heaven and will forgive their sin and will heal their land." ~ 2 Chronicles 7:14

From Vision to Victory

AS WITH MANY things, we have saved the best for last. The issue of prayer as it relates to the victory of God's people is so paramount that we couldn't simply allude to it and move on. There has never been, and will never be, true Christian victory where prayer was not an integral factor. Before we get into the depth of the praying life of Nehemiah, we need to understand some aspects of prayer that have become rather popular, yet unbiblical.

The first is that you can have a formula of prayer without faith. The idea behind this is simple: go through the motions of praying and that's enough. There are those who would advocate a prayer formula which deals with the function of prayer and involves no faith at all. Jesus dealt with this in the sermon on the mount, "And when you pray, do not keep on babbling like the pagans, for they think they will be heard because of their many words" (Matthew 6:7). This does not eliminate lengthy prayers, just prayers which are rote ritual with no real faith in Christ or relationship with God.

The Bible says in Hebrews 11:6, "And without faith it is impossible to please God, because anyone who comes to him must believe that he exists and that he rewards those who earnestly seek him." Again, in James 1:6-7 we read, "But when he asks, he must believe and not doubt.... That man should not think he will receive anything from the Lord." Prayer takes real faith, which is found in those who have a real salvation in Christ.

The second is that you can have effective praying without righteous living. God is not a divine genie who waits in heaven to simply do a trick for those who pray. God is more interested in your life being transformed, and those who are not living a transformed life run the risk of praying out of selfish motives (see James 4:1-4). 100%↑ ☺

There are those who might cause you to think that just the act of praying is enough to turn the heart of God. However, God requires holiness in a person's life for effectiveness in prayer. James 5:16b says, "The prayer of a righteous man is powerful and effective." Psalm 24:3-4 asks the question, "Who may ascend the hill of the Lord?" The Jesus

123

answer comes as such: "He who has <u>clean hands</u> <u>and</u> a <u>pure</u> heart."

The third is that your wants and not Christ's will is the focus of prayer. If you were to listen to many prayers that are offered in this day and age, you would hear people praying to have their own desires and will accomplished rather than their seeking after the heart and will of God. John 14:13 brings to light the <u>requirements</u> of <u>praying</u> in the <u>nature</u> and <u>character</u> of Jesus for the <u>glory</u> of <u>God</u>, "And I will do <u>whatever</u> you ask <u>in my name</u>, so that the <u>Son</u> may bring <u>glory to the Father</u>."

To pray "in Jesus name" is more than just tacking that statement on at the end of a prayer. It is to pray in the character of Christ – as if you're saying, "<u>I know this is a prayer Jesus would have prayed</u>." Again, in 1 John 5:14, "This is the <u>confidence</u> we have in approaching God: that if we ask <u>anything</u> <u>according</u> to <u>his will</u>, he hears us." *Responds*

Okay, now that we've covered what prayer is not, there are <u>four qualities</u> of praying that we will discover from the prayer life of Nehemiah. Prayer is the "golden thread" woven into the tapestry of <u>all</u> victorious Christian living. To go from vision to victory, <u>praying in faith</u>, in <u>righteousness</u>, and <u>for God's glory</u>, our prayers also ought to be:

Rigid, Defensive, Calvinist Authoritive Condescending Condemning

Passionate *Try Tears Jesus Loud Crying & Tears*

When was the last time you wept during a time of prayer? How about the last time you laughed, rejoicing in prayer? Have you ever had the experience of needing to pray so earnestly that you just dropped everything you were doing in order to pray? This might sound like a bold and harsh accusation but I fear that the life of many, if not most, of God's people are bereft of passion in their prayers.

For many, their prayers have simply become little more than mundane rituals of a religious life without any true desire or need on the part of the one praying. Simply put: it is just going through the motions. Now, before you get me wrong, I am not advocating emotionalism or the frenzied chaos some have called prayer, but I believe there needs to be a return to a deep and passionate life of prayer on the part of God's people. *Jn 15 Abide in Jesus Words*

Consider the prayer life of Nehemiah. In Nehemiah 1:4 you cannot help but get a sense of his passion, "When I heard these things, I sat down and wept. For some days I mourned and fasted and prayed before the God of heaven." He sat down and wept. He mourned and fasted and prayed. There is deep passion in the heart of this man when he prayed! He was, as some have called it, moved to prayer. The events and conditions of the world around him and the

Jesus played Offense 125" so we don't have to

information that Hanani shared with him caused a great stirring in his heart to seek after God. *Yahweh Nissi Yireh*

Until we are moved to passionate prayer in our lives, we will never truly experience great victories in our Christian walk. One of the truths of history is this: when God begins to draw His people back to a right relationship with Him, there is a great stirring in their hearts, a compulsion from God, calling His people to prayer. Consider the prayer of Manasseh, king of Judah:

Through much difficulty and distress - Thumping Down enter
Acts

In his distress he sought the favor of the LORD *Jesus* his God and humbled himself greatly before the *Reign* God of his fathers. And when he prayed to him, the LORD was moved by his entreaty and *Acted upon* listened to his plea; so HE brought him back to Jerusalem and to his kingdom. Then Manasseh knew that the LORD is God. ~ 2 Chronicles 33:12-13 *Elijah Yahweh is Elohim*

Great mercy
After all the evil Manasseh had done, and the wickedness in which he ruled Judah, even then his passionate prayer and repentant life moved the heart of God to restore Manasseh and return him from captivity back to Jerusalem. *Possession shalom*

The entire project of rebuilding the wall would have died except that Nehemiah was moved to prayer. So, what

Remained an ache in the heart of Elohim - Father found a man - the United Once Echad Father & Jesus & Holy spirit

The Passion of the Trinity for America — Appeal to Heaven GW @ ships

circumstances or events are surrounding your life where God is trying to call you to pray? Are you in distress because of sin and wayward living? James 5:13 says, "Is anyone of you in trouble? He should pray." Do not let prayer become nothing more than a religious token you hold up to God. It must be the passion of your life because victory is lost to those who are not passionate in prayer. *All in Consis's faith*

Purposeful *Join the Watch Until Jesus is Father in Heaven of Heaven is pleased & Satis Fied*

There is a downward spiraling trend in the manner with which many Christians pray today. Many prayers are steeped in meaningless generalities. We pray that God would bless this person or that person, or that God would provide for this missionary or that ministry. We pray these generalities simply because we have never truly understood the reality of praying with purpose. There is no victory to be gained through prayers that lack purpose.

Many Christians will tack on to the end of their prayers, "If it be Thy will." What that simply says is, "I have no clue what Your will is and I hope I have guessed it right." To pray with purpose is to pray in the will of God, and to pray in the will of God you must know the will of God, and to know the will of God, you must know God. Praying with purpose is then simply praying from the depth of your

Father's will is in the putting on the Lord Savior Messiah

relationship with God through Jesus Christ. If your relationship is not that deep, then your prayers are invariably without much purpose.

Again we come to consider the prayer and praying life of Nehemiah. Nehemiah knew the will of God, and thus he prayed accordingly. First, Nehemiah knew God's will was for the repentance and restoration of the people of Israel (see Nehemiah 1:6-7). For God's word to be fulfilled, Nehemiah then prayed that God would grant him favor in the presence of the king (see Nehemiah 1:8-11). Nehemiah prayed against the enemies who would try and disrupt what God was accomplishing (see Nehemiah 4:4-5). Nehemiah prayed that God would strengthen his hands for the work (see Nehemiah 6:9).

You will never find in the recorded prayers of Nehemiah any yielding to doubt or question concerning the will of God. He knew what God had called him to do and he prayed accordingly. He didn't pray with a sense of superiority over God, as if his prayers could command God to do anything, he simply prayed with confidence, knowing God would do as He promised.

So, how is your prayer life? Do you pray with purpose, having the confidence you know the will of God? The praying life of the early church, though not recorded

Request, Ratcrance
Read meditate   128
Resist
Forbid Close Loose Open

completely, gives illustration to the life of prayer the Apostles and others expressed.

> When they heard this, they raised their voices together in prayer to God.... Now, Lord, consider their threats and enable your servants to speak your word with great boldness. Stretch out your hand to heal and perform miraculous signs and wonders through the name of your holy servant Jesus. ~ Acts 4:24-30

And when they finished praying, the ground shook and God filled them with His Holy Spirit to empower them—in answer to their prayer! They had asked to speak with great boldness and God gave them what they needed to do so (see Acts 4:31).

Are you continually evaluating the circumstances around you according to the word of God and then praying as you hear from God's word? There are things happening all around us if we would simply open our eyes to the activities of God. When we do, we will know how to pray with purpose.

Personal

Much of the focus of prayer today seems to be centered on trying to make God aware of what is actually happening in life. Prayers go up to heaven as if God is clueless to the circumstances of mankind. But prayer is not our efforts to make God aware of our needs. God knows our need before we ask Him (see Matthew 6:8).

Prayer is not to make God aware of the circumstances of our life for God is aware of all circumstances at all times everywhere. Prayer is meant to bring us into harmony with God. Prayer is supposed to be personal in that it is the means by which we become involved in the nature and activity of the Almighty.

Look to the opening statement Nehemiah makes as he begins his prayer: "O LORD, God of heaven, the great and awesome God, who keeps his covenant of love with those who love him and obey his commands" (Nehemiah 1:5). There is no doubt Nehemiah wanted to make a personal connection with the Living God. In fact, in the end, when the project was completed, the very reality of Nehemiah's connection with God was realized as those who opposed him recognized that all of Nehemiah's activity was from God (see Nehemiah 6:16).

This is true even of the life and ministry of our Lord Jesus. At the grave of Lazarus, Jesus prayed so everyone would know that what was done was done within the relationship He had with the Father (see John 11:42). The truth is, victory is only gained when our prayers are built upon our personal relationship with God.

Think about this. Listen to the prayers you pray and ask yourself if your prayer is based upon your personal relationship with Christ and a determination to connect with Him in the matter at hand. Or are you praying a list of needs to the Father without even truly trying to come into communion with Him? Do you pray in recognition of God and His activity around you? Or, do you pray according to what you see you need without ever looking for God? Prayer ought to flow out of a deep personal relationship with the Heavenly Father.

Imagine if people communicated with their spouses the way they communicate with God. It would be a wonder that any marriage would last. The entirety of their communication would be a list of unfulfilled desires, demanding they be met with all haste. We say that no one would talk with their spouse that way, but that is how most of us pray: no relationship, no connection, just a list of demands and needs. How often do you pray just to express your love and devotion for Him?

Perpetual

Finally, prayer must be perpetual. There seems to be the notion that once something has been prayed about, its done being prayed about. Yet, even Jesus teaches a parable which shows the need to always pray and not give up (see Luke 18:1). Paul tells us to pray continually (see 1 Thess. 5:17). We must pray and continue to pray until we have received confirmation from the Lord that our prayer has been heard. We are in the midst of an era where fast everything is the norm. We have fast cars, fast food, fast communication, fast service, and even some fast churches.

However, prayer requires us to slow down and wait for God to do what God will do. We want everything in a hurry, including God's response to our prayers. It may just be that God is trying to teach us to pray and not give up.

Nehemiah continued to pray. There are seven different references to the prayers of Nehemiah in chapters one through six. I would venture to say, Nehemiah lived a continual life of prayer before God. This is a good indication Nehemiah knew that apart from a continual life of prayer, the work would never have been accomplished. Nehemiah prayed for encouragement, he prayed for strength, he prayed for deliverance, he prayed for protection, he prayed for success, Nehemiah just kept praying!

At this point some would ask, "How often do you pray?" I am not going to ask that. What I will ask is, "How constant do you pray?" Do you pray until you see the hand of God moving in the circumstances that surround you? Do you pray until you receive confirmation that you understand the will of God correctly? Do you pray until the peace of God, which passes all understanding, is guarding your heart and mind—your very passion and understanding? We open our lives up to a much larger experience when we finally give ourselves over to a continual life of prayer. Philippians 4:6-7 says, "Do not be anxious about anything, but in everything, by prayer and petition, with thanksgiving, present your requests to God. And the peace of God, which transcends all understanding, will guard your hearts and your minds in Christ Jesus."

The constant thread of prayer must be found in all Christian activity or victory will not be found. We may have some minor successes or some quick results, but true and perpetual victory only comes to those who will weave the golden strand of prayer into the tapestry of their lives. Prayer must be found with passion. It must be spoken with purpose. It needs to have that personal connection with God.

And, prayer must be perpetual. This, my friends, is the common thread of Christian victory!

Points to Ponder:

What circumstances have happened that indicates God is calling you to pray?

Are your prayers more like a "grocery list" rather than a desire to connect with the living God?

How constant do you pray?

Chapter Ten:
God is the Priority

"In that day you will say: "Give thanks to the LORD, call on his name; make known among the nations what he has done, and proclaim that his name is exalted." ~ Isaiah 12:4

From Vision to Victory

GOD IS IN the heart of victory! I think we forget this far too often in our Christian life. We have become success minded, purpose driven, growth oriented, and have precariously postured ourselves on the precipice of pride when we forget that it is God and God alone who grants the victory in the Christian's life.

One of the telltale signs a Christian is on the path of God's victory is that God is the one who gets the glory as well as the credit for success. Far too often we live within the framework of our own accomplishments. We take the accolades and applause and begin to believe we are the singular reason for the brilliance of our lives. We begin to think that we are doing God a favor by getting involved. Then, with self-importance so firmly established, we believe that our own will and desires are the very will of God. At the heart of it, we are prideful and self-involved, a people desiring the glory for our own actions rather than taking a back seat to anyone, including Christ. This can be seen in a myriad of areas, but one I would like to share as an example which happened some years ago in a church in Utah.

The church was growing and they wanted to build a new educational center. To do this, they needed to raise somewhere in the neighborhood of $100,000 over and above their normal giving. So, the leadership of the church decided they would sell bricks to place in a "walk of faith." That is, they would give people the opportunity to purchase a brick and have their names inscribed as one who belonged to the "walk of faith."

The plan succeeded and the money was raised. Now, who do you think received the glory and the credit for the accomplishment? Well, whose names are written all over the project? Certainly not God's name. No, the ones who received the glory were the ones who had their names set in stone. God received no credit, and the church members and leadership patted themselves on the back for a successful and ingenious project.

For Nehemiah, the rebuilding of the wall of Jerusalem was an accomplishment totally credited to God. Though we do not minimize the efforts of the people or the leadership of Nehemiah, the final victory is God's alone. I believe if

Nehemiah were standing before us today, he would declare this very thing: if it is to be a true victory, it must have God at the heart of it. When God is at the heart of our victories, three things will be evident.

God's Victory is Real

I believe the church suffers today from a sense of false victories. Let me create the scene. You enter the worship service, the music is playing and people are milling about. The preacher proclaims a message and emotions run high. The altar call is given, no one responds, and the service ends. Everyone goes back to their lives and the cycle repeats itself week after week. Surprisingly, many will say what an "enjoyable" time they had in church. Some might mention how they were moved (though not changed). Is that Christian victory? Is that what God has established the church to be?

There are many who work up a sense of victory in their lives and yet if you were to examine closely you would see that there was no true victory. They talk about how the word of God moved them—but their lives remain stuck in the mire of inaction. Many Christians talk about gaining victory in their lives over various temptations or difficulties or circumstances, yet very few actually talk about gaining

God in those areas of life. Why? Because their understanding of victory is self-motivated.

They want to be able to say they did something, they overcame, they conquered and so the victory and glory is completely theirs. Yet, if you were to go back and examine that person's life, you would see that there was no true victory, only temporary relief or momentary success.

For example, many people who are addicted to some substance have claimed to gain a victory over that substance. Yet in their lives all they have done is replace one addiction with another. From drugs, to alcohol, to gambling, to work, to sex, to whatever you can think of, they just transplant one problem with another. Now, is that true victory?

You must understand that God's victories are real. With God there is no ginned up hyperbole or exaggerated facts. When God does something, there is no doubt or question as to the reality of what happened. No one questioned whether Lazarus was raised from the dead (see John 11:43-44). No questioned that the man born blind regained his sight (see John 9:1-7). No one questioned that the demoniac of Gadara was set free (see Mark 5:15). They did question by what authority Jesus did these things (see Matthew 21:23), but there was no question He did them!

Here at the rebuilding of the wall, there was no doubt that the wall was completed, and completed in record time (see Nehemiah 6:15). In fifty-two days they were done with the rebuilding project and were ready to re-inhabit the city of Jerusalem.

With so many who claim a victory over something or in something or about something, and so few who call upon God within that something, it is no wonder the church suffers from a sense of false victory. Victory is not gained from a belief in something that isn't true until it becomes true; victory is gained by believing God for everything and doing what He commands.

God's Victory is Remarkable

The next reality is this: The victory God brings is remarkable. Not only is there no doubt the victory is real, there is no doubt that the victory was done in such a way as only God could do it. Go back to the story of the church that built their new educational wing. Was that remarkable? No. It was real, the money was raised and the wing did get built, but there was nothing remarkable about it. There are plenty of people who have enough pride in their heart to want to have their name engraved on a stone walk for posterity.

Victory that is remarkable is the death, burial and resurrection of Jesus. Victory that is remarkable is the preaching of Peter and three thousand get saved. Victory that is remarkable is the salvation of Saul of Tarsus becoming Paul the Apostle. As a matter of fact, victory that is remarkable is the salvation of anyone!

At the rebuilding of the wall, the people around the area considered the victory Nehemiah achieved to be rather remarkable. In fact it says this: "When all our enemies heard about this, all the surrounding nations were afraid and lost their self-confidence, because they realized that this work had been done with the help of our God (Nehemiah 6:16). Has your Christian victories been so remarkable that those who oppose you left in fear?

Let me ask a different question: have the victories of your life been such that no one could tell they were done by God? Or, have the victories that you've experienced been only the result of your own effort and ingenuity? If you were not sure what was done was of God, it probably wasn't.

I just wonder if we have given in to the attitude that there is nothing amazing about living by faith. So many Christians mull about with a half-hearted desire and meander through this life as if living by faith is mostly an unremarkable undertaking. But God has called us to walk in His victory – to join Him in His great enterprise and follow hard after Him so that the world will take note that we walk with Jesus. This brings us to our final point.

God's Victory is Revealing

The victories God brings into your life are solely for the purpose of revealing Himself — both to you and to a watching world. We often think we are the most important person in our relationship with God. Because of this, we tend to think God ought to do things which will bring us to higher places and greater glories. However, that is pride and will lead to the downfall of your Christian experience. God will not give His glory to another — including you (see Isaiah 42:8). But God does want to display His glory through you so that those around you can come to know and glorify Him (see Matthew 5:16).

Take for example, Lazarus. In John 11:40, Jesus speaks to Martha and says, "If you believed you would see the glory of God?" Here is another example to help you. Jesus and the disciples came upon a man born blind. The disciples asked if it was the man or his parents which caused this. Jesus said neither, but that the work of God would be revealed in his life (see John 9:3). Peter and John came along in the Temple and saw a cripple. "Silver and gold I do not have, but what I have I give you. In the name of Jesus Christ of Nazareth, walk" (Acts 3:6). The glory of God revealed, the work of God displayed, and the name of Jesus exalted — all of this comes as we live in the victory of God. Make no mistake, God's victories in your life are meant to reveal God, not you.

Though the victories of our life are meant to reveal the nature and character of God to the world around us, it does not mean that they will accept it. Consider what our Lord Jesus says, "If I had not done among them what no one else did, they would not be guilty of sin. But now they have seen these miracles, and yet they have hated both me and my Father" (John 15:24). And though the work of Nehemiah was clearly seen as done by God, the enemies around them still tried to intimidate them (see Nehemiah 6:19).

So, are you experiencing God at the heart of every victory in your life? These are the realities that make God's victories evident. First, they are real, not artificial. Second, they are remarkable, not undistinguished. Third, they are revealing of God, not you. If these realities are missing, then you are not living within the victory that is found in your relationship with Jesus.

From Vision to Victory

Points to Ponder:

What are the victories that God has done in your life?

Have the victories of your life resulted in praise for you or for God?

How has God revealed Himself through the victories in your life?

Conclusion
Living the Victory

"Shouts of joy and victory resound in the tents of the righteous: "The LORD's right hand has done mighty things!" ~ Psalm 118:15

From Vision to Victory

IN THE STORY of Nehemiah and the rebuilding of the wall of Jerusalem, we find a great and illuminating light shining on our own lives as well. God wants us to live in victory, to be ready to step forward and live such lives that the world must take notice of Jesus.

Throughout this book, you have read how to go from vision to victory. Now, at the end, I just want to encourage you to walk in the victory found in Christ. Consider the apostles as they faced the glaring opposition from the Sanhedrin. They stood strong and the men of the ruling council of Jerusalem took notice. "When they saw the courage of Peter and John and realized that they were unschooled, ordinary men, they were astonished and they took note that these men had been with Jesus" (Acts 4:13). Ask yourself this question: "who notices that you have been with Jesus?" Surprisingly, many people do if you are living out the faith and hope which is given to all who believe.

With the wall established, and the exiles returning, Nehemiah gathered them into the city square to hear the recitation of God's word. It was hard to hear, for they listened to the chastisements and judgments and understood all that was being said (see Nehemiah 8:7-9). However, Nehemiah reminded them of something else:

> Nehemiah said, "Go and enjoy choice food and sweet drinks, and send some to those who have nothing prepared. This day is sacred to our Lord. Do not grieve, for the joy of the LORD is your strength." ~ Nehemiah 8:10

Right now – this very moment – you stand in the path of victory, for God is victorious in Christ. Rejoice! Let your heart be glad, for the joy of the Lord is your strength as well.

Some might say, "But you don't understand the pressure I'm under." Let me say to you – Jesus understands. He has gone through the entirety of temptation and trial, everything mankind must go through, and has even shattered the barrier of death to bring victory for all who will follow Him. The writer of Hebrews tells us this:

From Vision to Victory

> Let us fix our eyes on Jesus, the author and perfecter of our faith, who for the joy set before him endured the cross, scorning its shame, and sat down at the right hand of the throne of God. Consider him who endured such opposition from sinful men, so that you will not grow weary and lose heart. ~ Hebrews 12:2-3

Don't lose heart, my friends. Jesus has blown open the door for all who believe in Him to find real victory in life.

Has God given you a vision of the life He has called you to live? Has He given you a purpose and direction to follow? Of course He has! It's all in the word of God, waiting for you to be faithful to read and discover His vision. If you want to know how to follow after the direction of God, to fulfill the vision and find victory, go back and re-read the principles that are illuminated through Nehemiah's project to rebuild the walls of Jerusalem.

I want to leave you with one final thought — a word of encouragement from the Apostle Paul:

> No, in all these things we are more than conquerors through him who loved us. For I am convinced that neither death nor life, neither angels nor demons, neither the present nor the

future, nor any powers, neither height nor depth, nor anything else in all creation, will be able to separate us from the love of God that is in Christ Jesus our Lord. ~ Romans 8:37-39

The security which is found in Christ Jesus is greater than all the opposition of all the forces of all the world. You are firmly fixed in Christ, if you believe, and now is not the time to shrink back from God's call. He has given the vision, step out in faithful obedience and discover that He has also provided the victory.

Points to Ponder:

Do you desire to live for Christ Jesus?

Are you prayerfully open to God's leadership in your life?

Will you step out in faithful obedience to do what God has shown you to do?

From Vision to Victory

150

From Vision to Victory

For more information about Michael Duncan and his books or to invite him speak at your event, you can find him at his website – http://www.michael-duncan.net

To listen to him on the Alive in Christ Radio Network simply go to – http://www.aliveinchristradio.com

To find him at his church, go to – http://www.mountainviewbaptistchurch.org

From Vision to Victory

152

Made in the USA
Coppell, TX
22 July 2020